# BECKY EXCELL

# GLUTEN FREE AIR FRYER

**Dedicated to my wonderful,
supportive and awesome
gluten-free community.**

# BECKY EXCELL

# GLUTEN FREE AIR FRYER

## OVER 100 FAST, SIMPLE, DELICIOUS RECIPES

**Photography by
Hannah Hughes**

quadrille

**WEEKNIGHT FAVOURITES 70**

**FAKEAWAYS 116**

**EVERYDAY ESSENTIALS 36**

# INTRODUCTION

**Imagine a helping hand in the kitchen that cooked your food faster (reducing the amount of time you spent in the kitchen), maybe even made it a little healthier, yet still delivered a finish you'd swear was deep-fried. Now imagine if it did all that but also reunited you with all the things you'd otherwise never eat again on a gluten-free diet. Oh, and what if I told you it would even do so at a noticeably cheaper cost than running a conventional fan oven too? No, I'm not describing the next generation of AI chef that cooks your food for you (though if it exists, sign me up!), I'm talking about <u>air fryers</u>.**

In case you hadn't already noticed, being on a gluten-free diet often means a whole lot more cooking and baking from scratch. Why? Simply put, it's because so many of the convenient options that we've likely relied upon for years suddenly become off limits. That includes everything from supermarket ready meals, packet spice mixes and ordering last-minute takeaways, right up to nipping to the bakery for a sausage roll or your favourite sweet treat. Even visiting your local coffee shop for a toastie or a bog-standard slice of cake (that you now realize you've wholly taken for granted) quickly becomes a whole new impossibility. If being gluten-free is still somehow considered trendy despite all that – something I've heard people say often – then I can only conclude that they're getting the word 'trendy' confused with 'hungry'.

Since I'm assuming that you don't currently hold the world record for holding your breath (and probably can't hold it until the above products and conveniences exist in an accessible, affordable gluten-free form), there's usually only one realistic answer to bringing them back into our lives: making our own gluten-free versions from scratch, at home. But wow, that sounds like a lot of time and effort spent on a sausage roll, doesn't it? And what if you don't even know how to cook your favourite Chinese takeaway dish or bake your favourite sweet treat, let alone how to make a gluten-free version that doesn't taste, well... gluten-free?

Luckily, this is where this book and your air fryer swoop in to save the day, armed with an arsenal of tried-and-tested gluten-free recipes and a trusty spray bottle of oil. Without question, these recipes and my air fryer have been the tag team that never fails to keep me reunited with more of the foods I miss – namely because I can now make gluten-free versions of my favourite foods in less time, using a boatload less oil compared to deep-frying, all while still achieving that unmistakable crispy, golden finish. Yes, that's right, this book assumes you don't have all the time in the world to cook. And all of that means both you and I can now make these recipes far more often! That's why I have absolute faith that the air fryer will bring back convenience to your now inevitable cooking and baking sessions, just like it did for me.

These (rather emotional) gluten-free reunions include all the foods I've already listed above and a mix of all the good stuff, from fish and chips to falafel, sweet and sour to spring rolls, doughnuts to dough balls, toad in the hole to turkey dinosaurs, and tons more. Best of all, with the right gluten-free air fryer recipes – which have all the gluten-free know-how and air fryer tricks built into them – you can recreate all the things you miss eating in a flash, but **nobody would guess they were gluten-free or made in an air fryer**. Naturally, these are exactly the kinds of recipes you'll find in this book. After all, when we already miss out on so much, why should gluten-free people have to miss out on air frying too?

And though I'm always over-excited to share all the glorious gluten-free reunions that these recipes will bring back to your plate, this book also promises to answer an often overlooked aspect of air frying: what on Earth do you serve alongside everything?

For example, what good is a recipe for golden, crispy, gluten-free air fried fish if you still have to switch the oven on for the chips (fries)? What's a gluten-free Chinese fakeaway without fried rice or prawn (shrimp) toast on the side? Or kofta kebabs without a flatbread? Whichever example you prefer, the answer is always the same: it's not a complete meal!

That's why this book is not only crammed full of recipes that'll guide you to gluten-free, air fried glory, but also includes a variety of exciting things to serve alongside them. See the Everyday Essentials chapter for mains and sides that are bursting with an eclectic choice of flavours; the Starters, Sides and Snacks chapter for 'super sides' as well as legendary savoury snacks; or head over to the Quick Breads chapter for easy must-have, yeast-free, bread-based heaven. Who could forget all the Sweet Stuff too?

So I hope you'll join me in yet another journey of gluten-free rediscovery through the magic of air frying, across over 100 recipes that you'll never stop making. Since a whole new galaxy of air fried gluten-free food is now ready and waiting for you, I'll let my air fryer conclude this introduction in the same way it lets me know that awesome gluten-free food is ready and waiting for me: **'beep beep.'**

# ABOUT ME

**Hello fellow air fryer enthusiasts! I'm Becky, I'm a gluten-free recipe creator, #1 *Sunday Times* best-selling author of five recipe books, with over a million of you following me across social media. If you've been following me online over the past few years, you might have noticed that I'm 'one of those air fryer people'.**

OK, first of all, I promise you it's not without good reason! While some might still think air fryers are a crazy fad that will eventually go away and see us all reverting to chucking everything in the oven, I couldn't disagree more. Not only because of everything I mentioned in the introduction but mainly because of how much value we've personally got out of our air fryer over the last four years in our home.

But when I say 'value', I'm not merely talking about how much cheaper an air fryer is to run compared to your average fan oven, though that's always welcome. I'm more alluding to things such as the amount of time our air fryer has saved us over the last few years. Or how the air fryer's undeniable crisping powers have allowed my boyfriend Mark and me to make more of the foods I miss – often unintentionally making them even healthier (than deep- or pan-frying) in the process. Needless to say, it has more than earned its place on my kitchen worktop, and that's quite an achievement considering there was never much space available there to start with! And I have every confidence that the air fryer will earn its place in your kitchen too.

The release of *Gluten Free Air Fryer* marks a big year for me as it's my fifteenth year of being gluten-free, and it's been a decade-and-a-half of ups and downs, to say the least! Being honest, I probably spent the first five years mostly struggling (not helped at all by simultaneously battling an eating disorder) and the subsequent seven or eight years reuniting myself with all the foods I missed, one by one, in my kitchen at home. But over the past few years of my gluten-free journey, I started to lack the one crucial element I always had plenty of in the past: time.

A lack of time meant that suddenly all the foods I'd worked so hard to recreate and bring back into my life had gradually become out of reach again. Although, of course, I still knew how to make them, finding the time to do so became a rarity; if I did have the time I'd likely be too exhausted at the end of the day for a spontaneous cooking or baking session.

If you've read any of my previous books or my blog, you'll probably already know that I've always had a zero compromise approach to creating gluten-free recipes. My mission has been to faithfully recreate gluten-free versions of the foods we can't eat so that the end result tastes exactly the same as the gluten-containing version, or in some cases even better. And that's because, if you'll allow me to stand on my soap box for a moment, I believe that gluten-free people shouldn't have to compromise on their favourite foods (or accept a lesser version) due to medical reasons that they have no control over.

So if, for example, the only way to enjoy proper takeaway-style fish and chips meant I had to create my own gluten-free beer batter and deep-fry my own fish and chips, that's exactly what I did. And judging by the number of times I've been out for fish and chips with friends and family only to be served a piece of fish without any batter, my kitchen at home is more often than not the only place I can actually conveniently enjoy the 'real deal'!

But sadly, I've learned the hard way that my zero-compromise approach on taste, texture and visuals can sometimes require more time than I can now actually afford. And though that approach never failed as the best route to the most authentic end product, it also meant that I had no choice but to make some of my most loved dishes less and less often over time. Strangely, I then started to miss those dishes all over again, just like I did when I first started a gluten-free diet all those years ago!

Fortunately for me, the time when I started to become time-poor was also when I bought my first air fryer. Back then there weren't many air fryer recipes out there, so it wasn't exactly an instantaneous solution! But as I used it more and more and began to understand how to get the best out of it, it quickly became my go-to, speedy route to all the foods I missed, often with less mess to clean up afterwards. Thanks to that trademark 'air fryer magic' resulting in a finish that can easily go toe-to-toe with deep-frying, I was still able to recreate all of my favourite foods while maintaining my zero compromise approach to gluten-free cooking and baking. Phew – what a relief!

If any of the above sounds relatable, then I can most definitely assure you that this is the book for you. And with it, I can also promise you that it won't take you fifteen years of struggling with trial and error in the kitchen and copious amounts of research before you can easily and conveniently enjoy all your favourite foods again, like it did for me. Speeding up every gluten-free person's journey back to normality has always been my mission, so it's my absolute privilege and pleasure to still be doing it here in my sixth book.

**<u>And if you were too lazy to read anything I just wrote above, then here's all you need to know:</u>** if a faster, easier and potentially healthier route to all the foods you can't eat on a gluten-free diet sounds good to you, then you've come to the right place.

Of course, don't forget to check out my blog (www.glutenfreecuppatea.co.uk) and my social media channels (@beckyexcell) for tons more air fryer recipes, with no doubt many more to come in the future.

**Happy air frying!**
**Becky x**

# AIR FRYER BUYER'S GUIDE

If you don't have an air fryer already and you're in the market for one, you might already understand how hard it is to know where to begin. Not only do they come in various shapes, sizes, finishes, capacities and brands, but the price can vary quite dramatically too.

Given that I now have three air fryers and have tested many more of differing shapes and sizes, all with different functions (I'm not that obsessed; it was for research purposes, I swear!), I've put together a no-nonsense buyer's guide, which will hopefully help you make your mind up.

## KEY THINGS TO CONSIDER

### Price

Prices can vary drastically, so this largely depends on your budget. Paying a little more generally nets you a machine that's likely to be more reliable, with a larger capacity, but these days there's no need to break the bank for an average-sized air fryer from a reliable brand.

### Capacity

Air fryer capacity varies from machine to machine and is usually specified in litres (or quarts in the US) – ranging from 2 right up to 22 litres (2 to 26 quarts), though something around 2–9 litres (2–9½ quarts) is more common. It's a good idea to think about how many people you'll be cooking for so you know how much capacity you need; for example, a 2–4.5 litre/quart capacity air fryer is fine for one to two people, and a 4.5–10 litre/quart capacity air fryer is better for two to four people, depending on what you're air frying. The more capacity, the more food you can cook at once. Otherwise you'll have to cook larger quantities of food in batches, which effectively means things take twice as long.

### One drawer or two?

While one drawer is most common at the lower end of air fryer pricing, some air fryers divide their total capacity into two drawers, allowing you to cook two things simultaneously but separately, at different timings and temperatures. However, some air fryers don't even have drawers – they instead open up like a grill (broiler), but in general the drawer design, whether one drawer or two, is more commonplace. If you intend to use an air fryer as a supplementary appliance to cooking using a stovetop and oven, an average-sized, one-drawer model should be fine for your needs. However, if you're aiming to cook entire meals using an air fryer, then a generous-sized, two-drawer model is the way to go.

### Brand

More expensive, well-known brands of course usually come with an increase in cost. However, from my perspective and experience, as these more well-known brands have a reputation to maintain, the products they make are more likely to last longer and be more reliable. Fortunately, some well-known brands make air fryers that are in fact very affordable, so if I had to choose between an unknown brand or a brand I've heard of or used before, I'd always recommend going with the latter.

## Worktop space

While air fryers don't tend to be huge, they do take up valuable worktop space, so it's important to get one that fits in with your space. There are lots of different sizes available, so please make sure you consider the measurements of the machine first – I might be stating the obvious, but the fewer drawers and less capacity an air fryer has, the smaller it will be.

Remember that air fryers shouldn't be pushed right up against a wall (they need breathing space behind) so ensure you factor that into your considerations about worktop space too.

## Digital screen

Some air fryers have a digital screen, which can make it easier to navigate, while others have two manual dials for timing and temperature instead. I personally like having the screen, as it makes everything very clear, but these only generally appear on more expensive models. I should also mention that some early models of air fryers don't even have a temperature control, it's just set at one permanent temperature and that's it! These days, any good air fryer will have temperature control, so steer clear of any that don't.

## Additional functions

As I mentioned earlier, many air fryers have features in addition to being an air fryer, so it's good to consider which features would be most useful to you. While some have bonus features such as roast, bake and reheat (which aren't life-changing by any means), some can slow cook/pressure cook, and some even double up as a full-on grill (broiler). I've also spotted (a rather expensive) one that's a microwave *and* an air fryer, which is even more game-changing, as it can replace your microwave and not take up any additional space.

## Noise

Air fryers are definitely not the quietest of appliances! They can get quite loud when they are in use, which could be something to consider, especially if your home involves open-plan living. I must admit that you do get used to it though! If I had to rate the noise, I'd say that the average air fryer is quieter than a hair dryer, but louder than a microwave. All air fryers generally create the same level of noise, but it's just something you should be aware of.

**Hopefully that should give you some idea of where to start, but don't forget to check out the FAQ section (overleaf) for lots more crucial info to your purchase too. Turn to the air fryer essentials section (page 20) if you're wondering which specific air fryer I use.**

# ULTIMATE AIR FRYER FAQ

Whether you're totally new to air frying or just want to learn more, this FAQ most certainly has all the answers you're looking for. These are all the questions I'm commonly asked online on a day-to-day basis, so naturally I've answered them in as much detail as I can here.

## HOW IS AN AIR FRYER DIFFERENT FROM A FAN OVEN? WHAT ARE THE BENEFITS AND DRAWBACKS?

Though I've already touched upon this in the buyer's guide (page 12), here's the long and short of what makes an air fryer an air fryer, as well as its benefits and limitations.

### Speed

Firstly, an air fryer is smaller than a regular fan oven, which means it has less air inside to heat; this of course means it heats up much faster (most don't need to even preheat) and cooks food more quickly. So speed is certainly the first difference.

### Smaller cooking area

Its smaller size allows it to heat up food quickly and preheat much faster compared to an oven, but then again you'll never be able to air fry your Christmas turkey in it (although I can fit a whole chicken in mine). So for particularly big families, you might find that you'll have to cook your food in batches or only cook one component of a meal in it if using a smaller air fryer.

### Crisper, healthier food

As air fryers blow hot air/steam out of the back while cooking, an air fryer creates a drier environment that allows food to crisp up better than in the oven, with less oil required.

### Cheaper to run

According to experiments done by some clever people, an air fryer is actually up to five times cheaper to run than a conventional fan oven. Depending on how much you use the oven in the first place, this could amount to a noticeable saving on your annual energy bill.

### Additional functions

Many air fryers have functions beyond simply air frying, depending on which model you buy. Common extra functions include a roast function, a reheat function, a grill (broiler) function, or in some cases the air fryer function is part of a multi-cooker, which can also pressure cook and slow cook too. So it really can be an all-in-one device that retires other small appliances entirely.

### Portability

Of course, air fryers aren't super light, but they are easy to move around the kitchen or transport in the car. For example, it would be easy for students to take a small air fryer to university with them, although it'll take up worktop space, which might make things awkward in smaller kitchens.

# IN TERMS OF CAPACITY, HOW MUCH DO I NEED?

If you're confused about capacity and how much you'll need, then remember this: I can cook a whole medium chicken (about 1.6kg/3½lb) in a 4.75 litre (5 quart) deep air fryer drawer, with next to no space left. With that visual in mind, hopefully you'll have some idea of how much food you can expect to fit in the average air fryer.

It's also important to know how that capacity is used in your air fryer: for example, a 4 litre (4¼ quart) air fryer basket could be very wide without much depth. In this case, it would be impossible to fit a whole chicken in it, but chips (fries) will cook more quickly as they'll be more spread out. Alternatively, another 4 litre air fryer's basket could be limited in width but make up for it in depth; this would allow you to fit an entire chicken in, but as other food (chips again, for example) will be more piled up, things will take a little longer to cook and require more shaking and turning throughout the cooking process. Neither is better or worse, it just depends on what you'll use it for most!

In my mind, it's better to have a little more capacity than you need, because if you get really into air frying like I unexpectedly did, you'll be able to do more without feeling the need to replace an already very new machine. Here's my general rule when it comes to air fryer capacity:

- **2–4.5 litre (2–4¾ quart) capacity:** Comfortably serves 1–2 people

- **4.5–10 litre (4¾–10½ quart) capacity:** Comfortably serves 2–4+ people

- **10 litre+ (10½ quart+) capacity:** You're ready for anything!

Of course, this depends on what you're making and is just a rough idea, but this book assumes your air fryer is around 4.5–10 litres (4¾–10½ quarts) in capacity.

# IS AN AIR FRYER HEALTHIER THAN DEEP-FRYING? CAN IT REPLACE A DEEP-FAT FRYER?

Yes, it is much healthier. When you deep-fry, you're submerging food in oil. When you use an air fryer you are using very little oil, yet can still get a lovely, crisp finish. The final product is not exactly the same as when deep-fried but it comes fairly close, with the added benefit of using a lot less fat.

However, it cannot entirely replace a deep-fat fryer, as foods coated in a wet batter (like fish coated in a traditional beer or tempura batter) will not work; the batter will stick to the basket or crisping tray and you'll lose it, or it will drip off before it cooks and sets. Wet batter is also much harder to spray with oil, because it just blasts the batter off; plus it needs a decent amount of oil, or the batter will be very pale and dry. Foods coated in a wet batter only generally work in a deep-fat fryer, which is why you never see these recipes cooked in an oven either. Because of this, I often just coat fish in breadcrumbs, crushed gluten-free cornflakes or flour instead, then spray with oil before air frying, for a similar experience.

# IS AN AIR FRYER WORTH THE MONEY?

As with every other kitchen appliance or gadget, it totally depends on how much you are going to use it. Each time you use it, you're getting value out of it. It's something that we use multiple times a week in our house and we now wouldn't be without it, so in our case, yes, it's definitely worth it. But if you are happy using your oven and feel no need for another appliance in the house (or don't have the space for one) then you definitely don't need to get one.

Of course, the more air fryer recipes you have ready to try, the more likely you are to use it – which is exactly why I wrote this book.

# IS AN AIR FRYER SUITABLE FOR A BIG FAMILY?

Air fryers come in all different shapes and sizes, but if you are a particularly large family, then even the average large air fryer would potentially not be big enough to cook an entire meal in one batch, solely in the air fryer. However, you would likely be able to make one or two components of a dish in the air fryer, such as crispy air fried chicken, while you boil your veg and potatoes for mash on the stovetop, for example; or you can always cook in batches while you wait for everything else to cook. If this is the case, bear in mind you'll need to keep the food that finishes first warm, or reheat it very briefly in the air fryer once everything is done. I usually keep food warm in a low oven until everything is done.

# HOW EASY ARE AIR FRYERS TO CLEAN?

It depends on your make and model, but in my experience they are very easy to clean using hot water and washing-up liquid (dish soap). With one of my air fryers (one with a lid that opens and shuts like a clamshell), I can simply throw the basket and tray into the dishwasher, no problems. This type of air fryer is the easiest to clean by far, and often air fryers that are also combined with slow/pressure cookers fall into this category.

But with the drawer machines, you shouldn't really put the whole drawer into the dishwasher as over time it'll likely degrade the plastic and handle on the front of the drawer. With my double-drawer air fryer, the instructions say you can put the drawer in the dishwasher, but it's 'not recommended for the longevity of the machine'. So basically, that's a no to me! Plus, water often gets trapped inside the plastic front of the drawer and slowly dribbles out after going in the dishwasher... which isn't particularly ideal. But of course, everything inside the air fryer drawer is non-stick so it's quite easy to wash up in the sink using washing up liquid anyway.

Don't neglect to clean the inside of the actual machine from time to time either (check the instructions on your machine for proper guidance) as there is always some splatter from cooking, which can burn over time.

## HOW COME YOU NEVER USE THE BAKE, ROAST OR SUPER CRISP SETTINGS IN YOUR RECIPES?

Though my air fryer has these settings, most air fryers don't. As I want my recipes to be usable for everyone in all air fryers, no matter how fancy they are or not, I refrain from using these settings in my recipes. Of course, you're more than welcome to use them and test them out yourself, if you have them!

## CAN I USE FOIL OR BAKING PARCHMENT IN MY AIR FRYER?

Yes to both – but please check the instructions of your air fryer for anything that says otherwise! However, the powerful fan that makes an air fryer super-effective at cooking also likes to blow things around. Not all air fryers have a protective mesh covering the heating element in the roof of the cooking compartment. If the foil or baking paper displaces and touches the element, the air fryer won't be able to work properly and whatever is touching the element will burn. To solve this issue, ensure baking parchment is trimmed to fit neatly under the food and that it's sufficiently weighed down. Make sure foil is tucked underneath the food if using it to cover items while cooking. Needless to say, never put baking parchment or foil into your air fryer on its own!

## YOUR RECIPES STATE TO 'HEAT OR PREHEAT' THE AIR FRYER. DO I PREHEAT MY AIR FRYER BEFORE ADDING FOOD, OR NOT?

The reason I state this is because one of my air fryers calls for a short preheating period that can't be avoided. If this is the case with your machine, simply allow it to do its thing and place the food in when it tells you to. Just bear in mind that if your machine does force preheating, your food might cook 1–2 minutes faster than my timings. However, if your machine doesn't call for a preheating period, like my main air fryer, you can simply put your food in and start cooking.

## CAN I COOK FROZEN FOOD IN AN AIR FRYER?

Generally, the answer is yes. In my experience, things like frozen chips, gluten-free chicken nuggets or fish fingers will cook about a third faster in an air fryer than the oven timings specified on the packet (just make sure you turn them halfway through and don't pile them up!). Chopped frozen veg works well too – simply air fry until fork tender. Avoid anything thick (like frozen chicken breasts or meat on the bone), which will only be 'air fryable' once defrosted. See page 33 for specific info on cooking common frozen foods in your air fryer.

# ESSENTIAL AIR FRYER EQUIPMENT

While having an air fryer is more than enough to get started, there are a few other handy things that will make your air frying life so much easier.

## Air fryer

Obviously it would be very hard to air fry without an air fryer... but the reason I mention it here is to mainly highlight this important point: I used a 9.5 litre (10 quart) air fryer with two 4.75 litre (5 quart) drawers that measure 15 x 20cm (8 x 6 inches) for all of the recipes in this book. Here's the brand and model for your reference: Ninja Foodi Max Dual Zone. If your air fryer is smaller than that, then no worries, but you might have to cook some of the larger quantities of food in batches. If your air fryer is reasonably larger than mine, then you shouldn't have a problem fitting everything in, but if everything is more spaced out and less piled up, you might find things cook even faster than specified.

## Silicone brush

Air frying isn't too dissimilar to BBQing in many ways, so it's not surprising that owning a silicone pastry brush is nigh-on essential here too. We'll mainly be needing it for applying marinades and sauces to meat and veg – however, it will come in handy in the sweet treats section for brushing on egg wash too. You can use a traditional pastry brush if that's what you have at home, but I use a silicone brush as I find it's far easier to clean and works better for marinades and sauces too.

## Tongs

I can't emphasize how useful a pair of tongs can be when removing food from the air fryer without damaging it, especially if your air fryer has particularly deep drawers. The sides and base of the drawer are also going to be scorching hot, and often a spatula is too large to be useful. So no matter what I'm cooking, I find myself reaching for these very regularly as they prevent a lot of burned/air fried fingers! But having said that...

## Spatula

Not the silicone baking kind, but the kind you'd flip an egg with. While its use is somewhat limited as it's often too big to take individual items out of the basket without squashing/damaging adjacent items, it does have its uses. It's great for lifting/flipping larger, whole items, such as chicken breast that's been butterflied (like the crispy parmesan chicken on page 82 or chicken katsu curry on page 123), steak or larger, flat fillets of fish and pizzas. It can also be used to gently prise anything that's a little stuck to the air fryer basket/crisping tray or for any situation where a pair of tongs would risk tearing whatever's stuck when lifted, leaving half your food stuck there!

## Digital food thermometer

As meat is a very common thing to cook in an air fryer, I'd highly recommend getting a digital food thermometer to check its internal temperature so you know whether it's done or not. As an air fryer cooks fast, it's quite easy to overcook meat to the point it starts to become dry, but with a digital food thermometer you can check the exact temperature and compare it to the handy internal cooking temperature chart on page 30. The only exception to this is generally when cooking meat like chicken thighs, which benefits from being cooked longer, or it can be a little chewy.

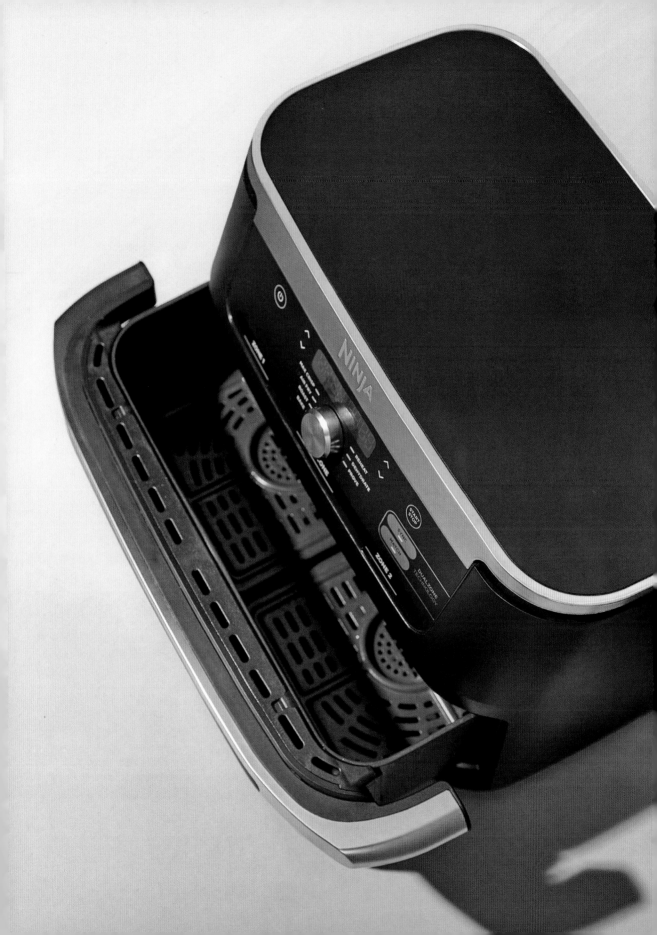

## Non-stick baking parchment

A good-quality roll of this comes in handy whenever you're baking from the Quick Breads and Sweet Stuff chapters. Not only does it provide a convenient cut-to-size base for your creations, but you can also use it to help lower things into the air fryer and vice versa. Ensure it's weighted down with whatever you're cooking, otherwise it can fly up into the air fryer's heating element and burn!

# BAKING TINS (PANS) AND CONTAINERS

## Foil containers or paper/silicone air fryer liners

For air frying wet batters, like when making Yorkshire puddings (page 182), American pancakes (page 206) or brownies (page 227), keeping that batter contained is absolutely key. Firstly, as the batter is wet, the air fryer basket or crisping tray becomes null and void... it has holes in it! The actual air fryer drawer/tray underneath is an obvious next bet, but can make wet batters hard to remove once cooked.

Cue foil containers (the kind you'd expect to see takeaways delivered in) and paper or silicone air fryer liners. All of them make it far easier to remove food from the air fryer without damaging the food within, while handily keeping your air fryer clean. You can find the foil takeaway containers in supermarkets and you'll easily find paper or silicone air fryer liners online, usually tailored to fit the common sizes of popular air fryers. Silicone liners are your best bet, as they're reusable and easy to clean.

## 10cm (4 inch) heatproof ramekins or pudding basins

These are conventional ramekins that I'd ordinarily use in the oven with reasonably high sides – an 8cm (3 inch) mini pudding mould works well here too. Their small size makes them perfect for using in the air fryer and they're essential for my chocolate fondants (page 220) and mini crumbles (page 223). These are quite common as they're often used for mini sponge puddings or soufflés, so look out for them in larger supermarkets.

## 15cm (6 inch) round baking tin (pan)

Though a conventionally uncommon size for baking as it's a little on the small side, I've found that it will fit into almost any air fryer without problems. You'll need this for my soda bread (page 195), air fried Victoria sponge (page 237) and brownies (page 227). I bought mine online.

## 10cm (4 inch) loose-bottomed or springform tins (pans)

I've had these in my cupboards forever and they always come out whenever I'm making small, individual-sized cheesecakes. Fortunately, they're absolutely perfect to use in the air fryer thanks to their compact size and, as they're springform, you won't struggle to remove the cheesecake without damaging it. I use these in my baked blueberry and lemon cheesecakes (page 228). I bought mine in the kitchen section of a department store a long time ago, but you can easily find them online too.

## Mini rectangular ceramic baking dishes (9 x 13cm/3½ x 5 inches)

These are yet another thing that you can easily find online and usually come in a set of four. The key difference with these is that they allow a wet mixture to be spread out a little more, which is super-helpful to ensure that whatever you're baking isn't under-done in the middle. I use these for my sticky banoffee self-saucing puddings (page 241).

## Silicone cupcake cases

In the absence of a muffin/cupcake tin (pan) that'll fit into your air fryer (most conventional ones won't) these are the perfect solution. Simply spoon your cake batter into a paper cupcake case, then place the filled case in the silicone cupcake case; that way, you won't need to clean them! These come in handy for my coffee shop cupcakes (page 224) and are available online.

# ESSENTIAL AIR FRYER INGREDIENTS

While in my previous books I list all the common ingredients used, here I'm just going to include the ingredients that are key to cooking and baking in an air fryer.

As usual, all of these ingredients are readily available in supermarket 'free from' or gluten-free sections, though you might need to hop online for tapioca starch. If you encounter any gluten-free ingredient not mentioned here, it's likely that's because it's a very common ingredient that you can find in nearly all 'free from'/gluten-free aisles.

## Vegetable oil in a spray bottle

**This is the most important note in this book!**
I'm going to be honest, having oil in a spray bottle is key, not just for air fryers in general but also for this book. Though air fryers are renowned for getting a crispy coating with minimal oil, how else would it be possible to get a light coating of oil on your food if not for a spray bottle? Answer: there isn't one... Fortunately, you can buy vegetable oil in spray bottles in supermarkets, or you can buy a cheap spray bottle online and decant your own oil into it – it's cheaper and the spraying action is usually better! Please ensure you read the 'don't' concerning low-calorie oil sprays in the air fryer dos and don'ts section too (overleaf).

Best of all, using a spray bottle is not only great for optimum dispersal of oil, but it's healthier and can save you money too. From my testing, I discovered that 20 sprays equates to just 1ml of oil - that's about ⅕ of a teaspoon. That means that when air frying, you'll end up using a lot less oil than the amounts you'd normally use in conventional cooking and a boat-load less than pan- frying or deep-frying!

**Side note:** For foods that are already coated in oil during preparation, such as in my air fryer chips/fries (page 38), there's no need to spray them with any additional oil.

## Gluten-free breadcrumbs

The reason I included this ingredient here isn't just because they are something I regularly use throughout this book. It's also because I need to mention that I use store-bought supermarket gluten-free breadcrumbs, which, in case you didn't know, aren't made from an actual loaf of bread! So, naturally, the results when using store-bought breadcrumbs vs using breadcrumbs made from a gluten-free loaf of bread can vary quite a bit in terms of taste, texture and visuals. While you can still achieve similar results with breadcrumbs made from gluten-free bread, you'll need to first blitz the (ideally stale and toasted) bread then potentially bake them too – you'll find a recipe outlining this in my first book, *How To Make Anything Gluten Free*. If you struggle to find gluten-free breadcrumbs in supermarkets, looking online is your next best bet. Failing that, you can always use the next ingredient instead...

## Gluten-free cornflakes

Though only essential for a couple of recipes (fish and chips on page 118 and katsu curry on page 123), I decided to include this ingredient here as, when crushed, gluten-free cornflakes make a great alternative to store-bought gluten-free breadcrumbs. And if you struggle to get your hands on gluten-free breadcrumbs, these would make a perfect substitute. Using crushed cornflakes instead of breadcrumbs certainly isn't a compromise, either; the golden, crispy coating they provide is absolutely divine. So feel free to use crushed gluten-free cornflakes if you'd prefer wherever gluten-free breadcrumbs are used in this book – just increase the breadcrumb quantity by around a third if using cornflakes.

## Gluten-free puff pastry

This ready-made pastry has been available in most supermarkets for quite a while now and cooks perfectly in the air fryer. I use JusRol gluten-free puff pastry, which is not only dairy-free but vegan too – so if using other brands, please make sure you double check it's dairy-free or vegan first, if needed. It doesn't puff quite as dramatically as the gluten-containing version, so do bear that in mind. Fortunately, the texture is absolutely perfect for my chicken balti pot pies (page 147), Eccles cakes (page 234), sausage rolls and veggie bakes (page 169), as well as my apple turnovers and hand pies (page 214).

## Gluten-free dried pasta

I'm sure you're already more than familiar with the dried gluten-free pasta you can find in supermarkets, but there's one thing you need to know before air frying any pasta dish: the pasta must be cooked in a pan on the stovetop first! It's not recommended to pour large quantities of water into any air fryer, so please don't be surprised when some of my recipes ask you to cook the pasta separately on the stovetop. If you find that your pasta breaks too easily when stirring it into other ingredients in the air fryer, either cook it to be al dente or use gluten-free brown rice pasta instead, which is much stronger but without any unwanted extra flavour. It's my personal go-to!

## Gluten-free white bread flour

As you probably know already, I'm a big advocate of supermarket-friendly gluten-free flour blends. Firstly because they're easily accessible, and secondly because the results speak for themselves! Unlike 'regular' bread flour, which is extremely high in gluten, gluten-free white bread flour isn't anywhere near as miraculous, meaning it can't be used as a like-for-like swap. However, the blend I use (FREEE by Doves Farm) has a decent amount of tapioca starch in it which, as you'll learn below, is a wondrous addition to any bread recipe. That's why you'll find the use of gluten-free white bread flour throughout the quick breads section in this book and beyond.

## Tapioca starch

You might be familiar with this white starch from my previous books and its best quality is undoubtedly the bread-like texture it brings to recipes. It's extracted from the roots of the cassava plant and crucially adds a little stretch to your finished baking products. That's why you'll find it in a handful of my bread and sweet treat recipes. This is one that you'll likely have to hop online to buy, but trust me – it's worth it!

I'm often asked if tapioca starch can be substituted for cornflour (cornstarch) and, on the whole, the answer is generally 'no'. When cooked, cornflour adds a sticky, jelly-like texture – you won't get any of the bread-like effect that tapioca starch introduces whatsoever. So if I call for tapioca starch as an ingredient, please make sure you include it – otherwise the results of your finished bake can vary wildly!

# AIR FRYER DOS AND DON'TS

You can't really go wrong with an air fryer, but these are my general dos and don'ts for using the recipes in this book, as well as air frying in general.

# DO:

## Bear in mind that all air fryers can vary in terms of cook speed and temperature

I've given timings for my machine here, but they may vary a little, especially if the capacity of your air fryer is smaller (if things are more piled up, they'll take longer to cook and need more regular shaking or turning over) or larger (things might tend to cook faster as they're more spread out) than mine, which has two 4.75 litre (5 quart) capacity drawers. Checking on your food regularly, especially nearing the end of the cooking time, is always a good idea, just to ensure things aren't getting overdone. With a digital food thermometer, you can check to ensure your food isn't underdone/overdone too (see page 30).

## Read your air fryer's instructions first.

I know it's probably quite boring and you just want to get started, but each machine varies so much depending on the brand, and caring for your air fryer will keep it running for longer, without a doubt.

## Grease the bottom of your air fryer where instructed.

If not, either your food will get stuck to the air fryer basket, or any coating on your food will get stuck there as well. It's also to ensure that the bottom side of your food gets a little oil too.

## Use your air fryer to cook frozen oven food.

Yep, you'll likely notice an improvement on the finish of frozen products too and, as most are coated in a little oil before being frozen, you usually won't need to add any extra oil to air fry them. Flick to page 33 for more info.

## Follow the cross-contamination advice on page 28.

Though the air fryer basket/crisping tray is usually easy to keep clean, the actual top part of the machine with the fan and heating element often isn't; this makes using an air fryer previously used to cook gluten-containing food a bad idea for gluten-free eaters. Due to the high speeds of the fan, any old crumbs could also easily be circulated into new food if they remain in the machine.

# DON'T:

## Be afraid to use oil, or try to use zero oil at all.

Yes, air fryers are healthier than deep-fat fryers because you can use a lot less oil, but using no oil at all is a sure-fire way for food to end up very dry on the outside. As air fryers have a natural way of removing moisture from the air, you need oil to ensure the outside is crisp, tasty and golden, not just dry, like sand! This especially applies to foods coated in a flour-based batter like Mark's sweet and sour pork or chicken (page 121) and my chicken zinger burger (page 138) where you need a little more oil than usual. Otherwise you'll be left with white floury patches that will burn. Using oil in a spray bottle helps us to use just enough and no more.

## Pile up food excessively.

A lot of the magic of an air fryer comes from the way the air is able to circulate around your food; if you pile it up, the food in the middle has no chance of getting that classic air fried finish.

## Cook using excessive liquid.

For example, boiling pasta in water is a bad idea, as the water could easily bubble up and boil over without warning, due to the high temperature.

## Cook things like popcorn or anything that could get blown into, and subsequently stuck in, the air fryer's heating element.

Light things like popcorn will really fly about in the air fryer, thanks to the powerful fan, and could get stuck in the very, very hot heating element. Needless to say, these will burn very fast and could yield potentially worrying outcomes!

## Keep food warm for too long by shutting it in the air fryer while it's turned off.

While it's very convenient to keep food warm in the air fryer until it's ready to serve, while the machine is off it won't be expelling the steam being created by the piping hot food inside. This means that anything that was nice and crisp when it finished cooking won't be after 5–10 minutes in this confined, steamy environment. Of course, you can always combat this by putting the air fryer back on to cook for a few minutes once you're ready to serve.

## Use low-calorie spray 'oil' and expect the same results.

There's only 50% oil in your average healthy oil spray, with the rest being water and thickeners. For air frying, the water content of these sprays isn't especially great for a crisp finish; I'd recommend just using less oil (in a spray bottle) instead of these low-calorie sprays. A crispy coating needs feeding with oil, otherwise (depending on what you're making) the coating might be crunchy... but only because it's rather dry – not necessarily a pleasant experience!

## Block the holes in the basket or crisping tray completely.

While this might seem similar to not overcrowding your air fryer basket, this point concerns baking paper more specifically. You might notice that I often instruct you to trim the baking paper around something you've just made before you air fry it. That's because baking paper is really good at preventing all air flow to the bottom of whatever you're air frying – to the point where the bottom of your food won't cook at all. So whenever I instruct you to trim that baking paper around something, make sure that you do!

# AIR FRYING AND CROSS-CONTAMINATION

The usual rules of cross-contamination apply to an air fryer just as they do whenever you're preparing gluten-free food. Although you should most definitely refer to the regular rules of cross-contamination in my previous books if you've never prepared gluten-free food before, in this book I'm only going to share the relevant cross-contamination info concerning air fryer cooking in particular.

**Firstly, I would highly recommend that you keep your air fryer 100% gluten-free to prevent all cross-contamination woes unless it's convincingly easy to thoroughly clean.** And by that I mean: don't ever cook any gluten-containing food in it... ever! As I've mentioned, though the air fryer basket is usually easy to keep clean, the actual top part of the machine with the fan and heating element often isn't; this makes using an air fryer previously used to cook gluten-containing food a very bad idea for gluten-free eaters. Due to the high speeds of the fan, any old crumbs could also easily be circulated into new food if they remain in the machine.

**Ensure everyone in the house is aware that the air fryer is a gluten-free zone.** In reality, foods made using gluten-free products in an air fryer are almost indistinguishable from those containing gluten. After all, most of the time simple swaps include gluten-free breadcrumbs, gluten-free cornflakes, gluten-free soy sauce and a little gluten-free flour, all of which will have almost no impact on the final finish of a dish. So, in short, there's very little reason for even gluten eaters not to abide by keeping the air fryer a gluten-free zone, as it barely affects the finished product anyway! If this can't be guaranteed, it might be worth getting a second air fryer that's strictly for gluten-free food only, and labelling it as such.

**Ensure all products and ingredients used are gluten-free.** This goes without saying, but it never hurts to have a reminder, does it? Here's a list of common sources of gluten that you'll need to avoid:

- **wheat**
- **barley**
- **rye**
- **oats**
- **spelt**

Of course, even if a product doesn't have any gluten-containing ingredients, it can still be cross-contaminated through manufacturing methods, so be sure to look out for any 'may contain' warnings and avoid those products too. Also, if a product is labelled as gluten-free and contains ingredients such as gluten-free wheat starch or barley, these products will have been tested to ensure they're under 20ppm (parts per million), the accepted limit for a product to be labelled as gluten-free in the UK. Note that the acceptable ppm limit can vary depending on where you live in the world, so check online for info relevant to your location.

**Ensure any utensils have been thoroughly cleaned before being used to prepare, cook or serve gluten-free food.** Dishwashers and washing-up liquid (dish soap) are fine for this. Ideally you'd have separate, brightly coloured or easily identifiable utensils and chopping boards for preparing/cooking gluten-free food. This is especially important when it comes to harder to clean items such as sieves.

# HOW DO I KNOW WHEN MY FOOD IS COOKED?

## Safe internal cooking temperatures

As I said in the essential equipment section (page 20), using a digital food thermometer is super helpful whenever you're cooking or air frying. With a digital food thermometer you'll never have to guess when your food is done or hack it to pieces to check if it's properly cooked; simply probe, read the temperature and compare it to the table here. It also comes in handy when reheating food in the air fryer, especially if reheating from frozen.

| FOOD | TYPE | MINIMUM INTERNAL TEMPERATURE |
|---|---|---|
| **Beef, lamb, pork and goat** | Steaks, roasts, chops (see page 67 for specific steak cooking times) | 63°C (145°F) Rest time: 3 minutes |
| | Mince (ground) meat and sausages | 71°C (160°F) |
| **Chicken, duck, turkey and other poultry** | All: whole bird, breasts, legs, thighs, wings, mince (ground meat), etc. | 74°C (165°F) |
| **Seafood** | All fish (whole or fillet) | 50–60°C (120–140°F) |
| | Prawns (shrimp), lobster, crab, shellfish | 63°C (145°F) Or at your own discretion |

## Air fryer cooking timings

And if you were ever wondering: how long do I air fry this for? Then here are all the answers you'll ever need to the most common questions. This information is a rough guide and can vary a little depending on:

- **How your veg, meat or fish is chopped (or if left whole).**

- **How spaced out or piled up the food is in your air fryer.**

- **Whether your meat or fish is cooked straight from the fridge or at room temperature (the following timings assume from the fridge).**

- **The make, model and drawer size of your air fryer.**

Despite these variables, this table should give you enough confidence to get friendly with your air fryer. To be certain everything is cooked properly, you can simply check that vegetables are fork-tender and use a digital food thermometer (and the safe internal cooking temperature chart, left) to confirm the done-ness of meat and fish.

All of these timings given assume you are using the standard air fry setting on your machine (not the roast or bake settings) and that you will shake or turn the food as needed to ensure all sides are evenly cooked.

# Vegetables

| FOOD | AIR FRYER TEMPERATURE | COOKING TIME |
|---|---|---|
| **Asparagus** | 180°C (350°F) | 10–12 minutes |
| **Aubergine (eggplant)** cut into 2cm (1 inch) cubes | 180°C (350°F) | 15–18 minutes |
| **Broccoli** broken into 4cm (1½ inch) florets **Tenderstem or purple sprouting** | 180°C (350°F) | 12–15 minutes |
| **Brussels sprouts** | 200°C (400°F) | 10 minutes |
| **Butternut squash** cut into 2cm (1 inch) cubes | 180°C (350°F) | 18–20 minutes |
| **Carrots** cut into batons 1cm (½ inch) thick and 5cm (2 inches) long **Baby carrots** | 200°C (400°F) | 18–20 minutes |
| **Cauliflower** broken into 4cm (1½ inch) florets | 180°C (350°F) | 15–18 minutes |
| **Cherry tomatoes** | 200°C (400°F) | 12–15 minutes |
| **Corn on the cob** | 190°C (375°F) | 16–18 minutes |
| **Courgette (zucchini)** thinly sliced | 200°C (400°F) | 10–14 minutes |

| FOOD | AIR FRYER TEMPERATURE | COOKING TIME |
|---|---|---|
| **Green beans** | 180°C (350°F) | 10–12 minutes |
| **Mangetout** | 200°C (400°F) | 8–10 minutes |
| **Mushrooms** thinly sliced | 200°C (400°F) | 6–7 minutes |
| **Parsnips** cut into batons 1cm (½ inch) thick and 5cm (2 inches) long | 200°C (400°F) | 18–20 minutes |
| **Red/green/ yellow (bell) pepper** cut into 2cm (1 inch) chunks | 200°C (400°F) | 10–12 minutes |
| **New potatoes** halved | 200°C (400°F) | 18–20 minutes |
| **Chips** 1cm (½ inch) thick | 200°C (400°F) | 20–22 minutes |
| **Potato cubes** 2cm (1 inch) thick | 200°C (400°F) | 18–20 minutes |
| **Fries** 5mm (¼ inch) thick | 200°C (400°F) | 15 minutes |
| **Potato wedges** 1cm (½ inch) thick | 200°C (400°F) | 20–22 minutes |
| **Onion** peeled and quartered | 200°C (400°F) | 15 minutes |
| **Pumpkin** cut into 2cm (1 inch) cubes | 180°C (350°F) | 18–20 minutes |
| **Sweet potato** 2cm (1 inch) thick | 200°C (400°F) | 18–20 minutes |

## Meat

| FOOD | AIR FRYER TEMPERATURE | COOKING TIME |
|---|---|---|
| **Bacon** | 200°C (400°F) | 8–10 minutes |
| **Beef burgers** | 200°C (400°F) | 10–12 minutes |
| **Beef or steak strips** | 200°C (400°F) | 8–10 minutes |
| **Whole chicken breast** | 180°C (350°F) | 12–15 minutes |
| **Chicken breast** cut into 2cm (1 inch) pieces | 200°C (400°F) | 8–10 minutes |
| **Chicken breast** butterflied | 200°C (400°F) | 8–10 minutes |
| **Chicken breast mini fillets** | 200°C (400°F) | 8–10 minutes |
| **Chicken drumsticks** | 190°C (375°F) | 22–25 minutes |
| **Chicken thighs** boneless | 200°C (400°F) | 12–14 minutes |
| **Chicken thighs** bone-in | 190°C (375°F) | 25 minutes |
| **Whole chicken** | 190°C (375°F) | 50–60 minutes (flip halfway) |
| **Chicken wings** separated at the joint | 200°C (400°F) | 16–18 minutes |
| **Hot dogs, frankfurters** | 200°C (400°F) | 8–10 minutes |

| FOOD | AIR FRYER TEMPERATURE | COOKING TIME |
|---|---|---|
| **Lamb chops** | 200°C (400°F) | 6–8 minutes |
| **Meatballs** beef, pork, lamb, chicken or turkey | 200°C (400°F) | 9–10 minutes |
| **Pork chops/ steaks** | 180°C (350°F) | 8–9 minutes |
| **Pork tenderloin** | 180°C (350°F) | 12–14 minutes |
| **Pork ribs** | 180°C (350°F) | 22–25 minutes |
| **Steak** based on sirloin (see page 67 for more info on cooking steak) | 200°C (400°F) | Rare: 7–9 minutes<br>Medium: 10–12 minutes<br>Well-done: 13–15 minutes |
| **Sausages** | 180°C (350°F) | 14–16 minutes |
| **Chipolata sausages** | 180°C (350°F) | 12–14 minutes |

## Other

| FOOD | AIR FRYER TEMPERATURE | COOKING TIME |
|---|---|---|
| **Large eggs** | 150°C (300°F) | Soft-boiled: 5–7 minutes<br>'Jammy' centre: 8–9 minutes<br>Hard-boiled: 10–11 minutes |

# Fish and seafood

| FOOD | AIR FRYER TEMPERATURE | COOKING TIME |
|---|---|---|
| **Prawns (shrimp)** raw and defrosted | 180°C (350°F) | 5–7 minutes |
| **Scallops** | 200°C (400°F) | 4–5 minutes |
| **Oily fish** e.g. salmon fillets and tuna steak | 200°C (400°F) | 9–12 minutes |
| **White fish** e.g. cod, haddock, basa and sea bass fillets | 200°C (400°F) | 8–10 minutes |

# Frozen food

These timings are given for common frozen-aisle products and free-from frozen products, assuming you're air frying them straight from frozen. There's no need to add any extra spray oil to any of these, but greasing the base of your air fryer when cooking breadcrumbed or battered products is advised to ensure they don't stick.

| FROZEN FOOD | AIR FRYER TEMPERATURE | COOKING TIME |
|---|---|---|
| **Bread** sliced | 200°C (400°F) | 4–5 minutes |
| **Bread roll** | 180°C (350°F) | 10 minutes |
| **Calamari** | 200°C (400°F) | 10–12 minutes |
| **Chicken nuggets** | 180°C (350°F) | 14–16 minutes |
| **Chips, French fries or wedges** | 200°C (400°F) | 14–16 minutes |

| | | |
|---|---|---|
| **Fish fillets** battered or breadcrumbed | 200°C (400°F) | 12–14 minutes |
| **Fish or veggie fingers** | 200°C (400°F) | 10–12 minutes |
| **Pizza** | 200°C (400°F) | 10–12 minutes |
| **Scampi** | 200°C (400°F) | 12–14 minutes |
| **Veggie burgers + sausages** | 200°C (400°F) | 10–12 minutes |
| **Sausages** | 180°C (350°F) | 14–16 minutes |
| **Burgers** | 200°C (400°F) | 12–14 minutes |

# Oven temperature conversions:

Not sure how to cook your favourite oven-based recipe in the air fryer? The chart below should give you a rough starting point of the temperature conversions you'll need to make. This can also be handy if you're trying to reverse-engineer an air fryer recipe to prepare it in the oven too.

| OVEN | FAN OVEN | AIR FRYER |
|---|---|---|
| 190°C (375°F) | 170°C (340°F) | 150°C (300°F) |
| 200°C (400°F) | 180°C (350°F) | 160°C (325°F) |
| 210°C (410°F) | 190°C (375°F) | 170°C (340°F) |
| 220°C (425°F) | 200°C (400°F) | 180°C (350°F) |
| 230°C (450°F) | 210°C (410°F) | 190°C (375°F) |
| 240°C (465°F) | 220°C (425°F) | 200°C (400°F) |

# KEY

Just as a handy reminder for those still in disbelief: yes, everything in this entire book is gluten-free, as well as air fryer friendly!

But it's also incredibly important to me that as many people can enjoy my recipes as possible. That's why I've labelled all of my recipes to clearly indicate whether they're dairy-free, lactose-free, low lactose, vegetarian, vegan or low FODMAP.

Even if a recipe isn't naturally suitable for all dietary requirements, watch out for the helpful notes by the key. These will indicate any simple swaps you can implement in order to adapt that recipe to your dietary requirements, if possible.

**For recipes that have '3 ways'** – meaning three different variations (such as those in the Essentials chapter, overleaf) – the presence of <u>any</u> of the dietary keys means all three recipe variations are suitable for that diet <u>unless</u> the notes next to the key specifically instruct you to only make one/two named variation(s). However, if one of the recipe variations only needs a simple swap or two to make it suitable for the diet in question, that advice will be written next to the key instead, including which specific variation(s) need adapting.

**Here's a breakdown of the labels I'll be using so you know what they look like and exactly what I mean when I use them:**

##  Dairy-free

This indicates that a recipe contains zero dairy products. Ensure that no ingredients used have a 'may contain' warning for traces of dairy and double-check that everything used is 100% dairy-free. Please ensure all ingredients and any convenience products used are dairy-free, such as cocoa powder.

## LF Lactose-free

Lactose-free? Isn't that the same as dairy-free? No, it definitely isn't! For example, lactose-free milk is *real* cow's milk with the lactase enzyme added, so while it's definitely not dairy-free, it is suitable for those with a lactose intolerance. The 'lactose-free' label indicates that a recipe is naturally lactose-free or uses lactose-free products. Please ensure all ingredients and any convenience products used are lactose-free.

## LL Low lactose

Ingredients like butter and harder cheeses (such as Cheddar and Parmesan) are incredibly low in lactose. That means that people with a lactose intolerance should have no problems tolerating them. So for those ingredients, you won't necessarily need a special 'lactose-free' equivalent. Of course, recipes that use these ingredients aren't technically 'lactose-free', so they'll be labelled as low lactose for clarity. Please ensure all ingredients and any convenience products used are lactose-free or very low in lactose.

## V Vegetarian

This indicates that a recipe is both meat-free and fish-free. I've provided simple veggie swaps where necessary and possible. Please make sure any products and ingredients used are vegetarian-friendly.

## VE Vegan

This indicates that a recipe contains no ingredients that are derived from animals. Please ensure all ingredients and any convenience products used are vegan-friendly.

#  Low FODMAP

This indicates that one serving of the finished recipe is low FODMAP. The low FODMAP diet was specifically created by Monash University in order to help relieve the symptoms of IBS in sufferers.

**A couple of quick side notes:**

Whenever I mention spring onions (scallions) in this book, I mean the green parts <u>only</u> for FODMAP reasons. Also, garlic-infused oil is low FODMAP, as long as it's clear and doesn't have visible bits of garlic floating in it. Ensure any products used (such as spices, seasonings or sausages, for example) are free of onion and garlic powder – these tend to be common ingredients in spice blends. You'll easily find low FODMAP convenience products – such as stock cubes and curry powder – online.

Some ingredients, such as red (bell) pepper, have specific low FODMAP serving sizes – in this case it's 43g (1½oz) . In recipes where red pepper is used but this low FODMAP serving size weight isn't mentioned, that'll be because once you divide the finished dish between the amount of people it serves, the amount of red pepper in each serving per person will be under 43g (1½oz). However, if you use an absolutely huge red pepper, use more peppers than specified, or enjoy more than the specified serving size per person, this might then exceed the safe FODMAP serving size limit; in this case, you should first weigh out how much red pepper you need before you start the recipe to ensure a safe serving size of 43g (1½oz) per person. Alternatively, you can use a green pepper instead, which has a higher FODMAP serving size of 75g (2⅔oz).

**Brief disclaimer:** You should always start the low FODMAP diet in consultation with your dietician. Please ensure all ingredients and any convenience products used are low FODMAP. All FODMAP serving sizes were correct at the time of writing. As Monash University regularly tests the FODMAP levels of different foods, these quantities might change over time as new research emerges. For example, in my previous books the low FODMAP serving size given for avocado was 30g (1oz), but new research by Monash University means this has now been updated to 60g (2¼oz). Be sure to check their website every now and then for the latest info.

# ❄ Freezable

This indicates that the prepared ingredients or finished product is freezable. Look out for a note next to this key, which will tell you how long you can freeze a dish for, whether you can air fry it straight from frozen or if it will need to be thawed first, plus any cooking time adjustments. Of course, make sure that you store everything in an airtight container or freezer bags before freezing. Oh, and don't forget to label and date anything you freeze to avoid that not-so-fun freezer game: 'what even is this?' If there is no freezer symbol present, that means I don't recommend freezing the recipe.

# EVERYDAY ESSENTIALS

Meet the chapter where, even if you only used your air fryer for these recipes and not much else, you'd still be well on your way to getting your money's worth out of it. That's because these are all beginner-friendly family favourites that will easily pair with your existing regular meals. They are so simple and quick to make, you'll find yourself making them again and again… and again!

Though this chapter aims to tackle all the basic, common things we all love to cook in an air fryer, it is also a well of inspiration for transforming these classic dishes into wow-inducing centrepieces and super sides. That's why I decided to do each recipe in this chapter three different ways, giving you choice and variety in addition to the core cooking instructions and timings.

As I've said before, being gluten-free often means spending more time in the kitchen cooking from scratch but, fortunately, these recipes never fail to massively reduce that time and always result in a crisper, crunchier finish than if done in the oven.

So whether you're new to air frying, or are seeking examples of how you might use your air fryer in your day-to-day cooking routine, then look no further.

# CRISPY CHIPS 3 WAYS

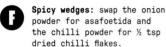

**Spicy wedges:** swap the onion powder for asafoetida and the chilli powder for ½ tsp dried chilli flakes.

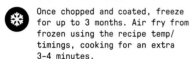

Once chopped and coated, freeze for up to 3 months. Air fry from frozen using the recipe temp/timings, cooking for an extra 3–4 minutes.

- 600g (1lb 5oz) Maris Piper potatoes, skin on or off
- 3 tbsp vegetable or olive oil
- 1 tsp salt
- ½ tsp ground black pepper
- 2 tbsp gluten-free plain (all-purpose) flour or cornflour (cornstarch)

**For Chinese takeaway-style salt and pepper chips**

- ½ tsp Chinese five spice
- ½ tsp ground ginger
- ½ tsp dried chilli flakes

**For rosemary salted fries**

- 2 sprigs of fresh rosemary or 1 tbsp dried

**For spicy wedges**

- ½ tsp onion powder
- 1 tsp chilli powder
- 1 tsp smoked paprika
- Pinch of ground turmeric

**Serves 2–3 / Takes 20–25 minutes**

**Here's how to transform a humble bag of spuds into gloriously crispy chips, French fries or chunky wedges. Adding a little gluten-free flour creates a foolproof light and crispy coating – a trick I learned from all the best-looking frozen supermarket chips, which are never gluten-free. Either enjoy your chips/fries/wedges with a little salt and pepper or add one of three seasoning choices. For two-drawer air fryers, I'd highly recommend splitting the chips between both drawers for speed and the crispest finish.**

**For chips:** Cut the potatoes into strips 1cm (½ inch) wide and 5mm (¼ inch) thick.

**For fries:** Use a mandoline on the widest, most open setting, which should be around 5mm (¼ inch). If your mandoline has a blade specifically for French fry shapes, then attach that blade and slice away. If not, simply use the straight mandoline blade to cut disc shapes, then use a large, sharp knife to slice each disc into 5mm (¼ inch) wide fries.

**For wedges:** Cut each potato into quarters, then slice at an angle into wedges; the thickest part should be no thicker than 1cm (½ inch). To prevent your wedges being huge, it's best to use multiple apple-sized potatoes rather than fewer enormous ones.

Add the prepared potatoes to a medium bowl, followed by the oil, salt and pepper. Mix until well coated, then add the flour and your seasoning mix of choice. Mix until the flour disappears, ensuring that no potato pieces are stuck together. Heat or preheat the air fryer to 200°C/400°F.

Place the potatoes in the air fryer basket and air fry for 15–22 minutes until browned at the edges and crisp, turning them over halfway through and separating any that are stuck together. Chips and wedges will take closer to 22 minutes while French fries should be done in around 15 minutes.

**continued overleaf**

Serve alongside your favourite dinners, such as my cornflake-crusted fish and chips (page 118), salmon burgers (page 88), zinger burger (page 138), bean burgers (page 96) or steak (page 67).

## TIPS

Remember, the key to crispy chips/fries/wedges is to ensure they're not piled up too much and are well shaken/regularly turned in the air fryer basket. Oh, and the oil in the coating helps out a lot too, so don't scrimp there!

Ensure all the potatoes are cut to be as uniform in size as possible. If not, smaller/thinner pieces will cook and burn before larger/thicker pieces are done.

A cooking mandoline is a kitchen gadget that you can easily buy in supermarkets or online. Essentially, it's created to make slicing vegetables super-quick and easy and, best of all, it helps to create consistent slices that are all the same thickness – perfect for ensuring your fries all cook evenly and at the same time! Use with care though: the blade is very sharp so be especially wary when slicing small chunks of veg that are hard to grip. If your mandoline comes with a guard and/or protective gloves, do use them!

# SWEET POTATO 3 WAYS

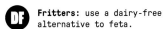

**Fritters:** use a dairy-free alternative to feta.

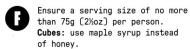

Ensure a serving size of no more than 75g (2½oz) per person.
**Cubes:** use maple syrup instead of honey.

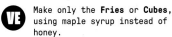

Make only the **Fries** or **Cubes**, using maple syrup instead of honey.

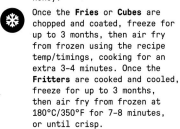

Once the **Fries** or **Cubes** are chopped and coated, freeze for up to 3 months, then air fry from frozen using the recipe temp/timings, cooking for an extra 3-4 minutes. Once the **Fritters** are cooked and cooled, freeze for up to 3 months, then air fry from frozen at 180°C/350°F for 7-8 minutes, or until crisp.

- 3 medium-sized sweet potatoes (700g/1lb 8½oz in total)
- Vegetable oil in a spray bottle, for greasing

**For sweet potato fries**
- 3 tbsp vegetable or olive oil
- 1 tbsp smoked paprika
- 1 tsp salt
- ½ tsp ground black pepper
- 4 tbsp gluten-free plain (all-purpose) flour or cornflour (cornstarch)

**For hot honey sweet potato cubes**
- 3 tbsp vegetable or olive oil
- 3 tbsp honey
- 1 tsp dried chilli flakes, plus a little extra to serve
- 2 tsp apple cider vinegar
- 1 tsp salt
- 4 tbsp gluten-free plain (all-purpose) flour or cornflour (cornstarch)

**continued overleaf**

Serves 2-3 / Takes 25 minutes

**Welcome to my three go-to ways to serve sweet potatoes, all of which I will never be making in the oven again! The inclusion of gluten-free flour in each of these variations plays an important role in ensuring a crisp finish (as well as binding in the fritters) as sweet potatoes just don't crisp up like potatoes do. You'll only need to peel the sweet potatoes to make fritters, otherwise it's totally up to you whether you leave the skin on or not – I usually leave it on for added texture and flavour.**

**For fries:** Cut the sweet potatoes into strips 1cm (½ inch) wide and 5mm (¼ inch) thick. Add the fries to a medium bowl, followed by the oil, smoked paprika, salt and pepper. Mix until well coated, then add the flour and mix once more.

**For cubes:** Chop the sweet potato into 2cm (¾ inch) cubes and transfer to a medium bowl. Add the oil, honey, chilli flakes, vinegar and salt. Mix until well coated, then add the flour and mix once more.

Heat or preheat the air fryer to 200°C/400°F. Generously grease the base of the air fryer basket or crisping tray by spraying it with oil.

Place the fries or cubes in the air fryer basket (making sure they're touching as little as possible) and spray once more with oil. Air fry for 18–20 minutes until browned at the edges, turning over halfway through or shaking 3 or 4 times if particularly piled up.

**For fritters:** Peel and grate the sweet potato; a food processor with the grating attachment can massively speed up this process! Squeeze out as much liquid as you can from the grated sweet potato if it's particularly soggy and place in a large bowl.

Add the feta, paprika, chives, salt, pepper and eggs, then mix well. Add the flour and mix once more until fully combined and the flour disappears. Use your hands to form patties and place them on a board or large plate.

**continued overleaf**

**For sweet potato fritters**
- 200g (7oz) feta, crumbled
- 2 tbsp smoked paprika
- Large handful of chives, finely chopped
- 2 tsp salt
- 1 tsp ground black pepper
- 4 medium eggs
- 100g (¾ cup) gluten-free plain (all-purpose) flour
- Lime wedges, for squeezing (optional)

Heat or preheat the air fryer to 180°C/350°F. Generously grease the base of the air fryer basket or crisping tray by spraying it with oil. Transfer as many patties into the air fryer as will comfortably fit without touching, then spray each with oil.

Air fry for 12–14 minutes until they have a crisp exterior and are cooked through, flipping over and spraying with a little more oil halfway through.

Serve your fries/cubes/fritters with lime wedges for squeezing (if you like) alongside your favourite dinners, such as my fish cakes (page 85), chicken wings (page 59), salmon (page 62) or turkey dinosaurs (page 103).

### TIP

The more spread out your sweet potato fries or cubes are in the air fryer (and the less they're touching), the easier it is to achieve that crispy finish. If you have an air fryer with two drawers, I'd highly recommend splitting them between both. Or simply cook in batches.

# CRISPY 'ROAST' POTATOES 3 WAYS

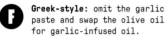

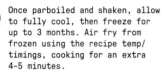

**Greek-style:** omit the garlic paste and swap the olive oil for garlic-infused oil.

Once parboiled and shaken, allow to fully cool, then freeze for up to 3 months. Air fry from frozen using the recipe temp/timings, cooking for an extra 4-5 minutes.

- 1kg (2lb 3oz) Maris Piper potatoes, peeled and chopped into 2.5cm (1 inch) chunks
- Vegetable oil in a spray bottle, for greasing

**For classic roast potatoes**
- 4 tbsp olive oil
- 1 tsp salt

**For Greek-style lemon and garlic roast potatoes**
- 4 tbsp olive oil
- 1 tsp garlic paste
- Grated zest of 1 small lemon and juice of ½
- 1 tbsp dried oregano
- 1 tsp salt
- ½ tsp ground black pepper

**For rosemary salted potatoes**
- 4 tbsp olive oil
- 2 sprigs of fresh rosemary or 1 tbsp dried
- 1 tsp flaky salt, plus an extra pinch to serve

**Serves 4-5 / Takes 35 minutes**

**Having tested both parboiling and not parboiling my roast potatoes before air frying, I'm happy to report that parboiling and shaking them first resulted in spuds as good as roasting them in the oven, if not better, with far less oil. So that's exactly the method I'm providing here. Whether you opt for classic, Greek-style or rosemary salted roast potatoes, expect super-crispy, crunchy roast potatoes every time that everyone will be raving about.**

Bring a large saucepan of salted water to the boil on the stove, then add the chopped potatoes. Boil for about 10 minutes, starting from the point at which the water is bubbling. The potatoes should be soft on the outside but firm in the middle.

Drain and transfer the potatoes back to the saucepan. Add all the other ingredients, depending on which variation you are making.

Pop the lid on the saucepan and shake a good few times to fluff up the outside of the potatoes. This helps to give them a crispy exterior once air fried.

Heat or preheat the air fryer to 200°C/400°F. Generously grease the base of the air fryer basket or crisping tray by spraying it with oil.

Place the potatoes in the air fryer basket, making sure they're in a single layer and touching as little as possible. You'll likely have to cook them in batches so as not to overcrowd things if your air fryer doesn't have enough space. Air fry for 18–20 minutes, turning them over at least twice during the cooking time. For rosemary salted potatoes, sprinkle over an extra pinch of salt before serving.

Serve with a roast dinner centrepiece, like my toad in the hole (page 81), whole chicken (page 56), cauliflower steaks (page 52) or pork steaks (page 65), alongside air fryer Yorkshire puddings (page 182) with lots of gluten-free gravy.

**continued overleaf**

**TIP**

For two-drawer air fryers, it's essential that you split the parboiled and shaken potatoes between both drawers for speed and the crispest finish – this is a lot of potato and piling it all up in one drawer is not going to achieve great results! If you must use just one drawer, simply cook the full quantity in two batches.

# POTATOES 3 WAYS

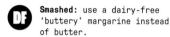

**Smashed:** use a dairy-free 'buttery' margarine instead of butter.

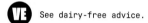

See dairy-free advice.

Once cooled, freeze for up to 3 months. Air fry from frozen at 200°C/400°F: 8-10 minutes for **Hasselback** or **Smashed**, 20-22 minutes for **Jacket**.

## For classic jacket potatoes
- 2 medium Russet or Yukon Gold baking potatoes, skin on
- 1 tbsp olive oil
- Pinch of flaky sea salt
- ¼ tsp ground black pepper

## For gunpowder hasselback potatoes (pictured overleaf)
- 600g (1lb 5oz) baby potatoes, skin on
- 3 tbsp garlic-infused oil
- 1 tsp garam masala
- ½ tsp dried chilli flakes or Kashmiri chilli flakes
- ½ tsp dried fenugreek
- ½ tsp salt
- Small handful of coriander (cilantro), finely chopped, to serve

## For smashed potatoes
- 6-7 small-medium Maris Piper or King Edward potatoes (600g/ 1lb 5oz total), skin on
- 1 tbsp butter
- 1 tbsp olive oil
- 1 tsp salt
- ½ tsp ground black pepper
- Vegetable oil in a spray bottle, for greasing

**Serves 2 / Takes 25 minutes + cooling**

**Whether you fancy a jacket potato ready to top for lunch or crispy hasselback/smashed potatoes as a super side for dinner, a tag team between the air fryer and microwave is key. The microwave ensures they're perfectly cooked and fluffy in the middle and the air fryer gives the skin a perfectly crisp crunch – just ensure you let the potatoes partially cool before air frying first. Oh, and bear mind you'll need slightly different sizes and varieties of potatoes depending on the variation you've chosen for this recipe.**

**For classic jacket potatoes:** Pierce the potatoes all over with a fork, wrap in kitchen paper, place on a plate and microwave for 10 minutes (900W). Once done, you should be able to easily pierce them with a skewer all the way through without resistance. Discard the kitchen paper and allow to cool for 20 minutes (or the skin won't crisp up as much).

Heat or preheat the air fryer to 200°C/400°F.

Brush or spray each potato with the olive oil on all sides and sprinkle with the salt and black pepper. Place in the air fryer basket and air fry for 15 minutes until golden and crisp, turning them over halfway through.

Serve with your choice of classic jacket potato toppings and a side salad, or serve as a side alongside my chicken balti pie (page 147), fish cakes (page 85) or chicken Kyivs (page 110).

**For gunpowder hasselback potatoes:** Heat or preheat the air fryer to 180°C/350°F.

Make multiple slits into each potato without cutting all the way through. The easy way to do this is by placing each potato in the recessed part of a wooden spoon. Using a sharp knife, cut deep slits across each potato and the spoon should prevent you from cutting all the way through.

**continued overleaf**

Place in a suitably sized microwave-safe bowl and loosely cover with a plate. Microwave for 6 minutes (900W) then allow to cool for 20 minutes (or the skin won't crisp up as much).

Add the garlic-infused oil, garam masala, chilli flakes, fenugreek and salt to the bowl. Stir briefly until everything is well coated.

Heat or preheat the air fryer to 180°C/350°F. Place the potatoes in the air fryer, ensuring there is generous space between them, and air fry for 22–25 minutes, turning over halfway through. Smaller baby potatoes will cook in 22 minutes, but the larger ones will finish closer to 25 minutes.

To serve, sprinkle with chopped coriander and serve alongside honey mustard salmon (page 62), tandoori whole chicken (page 56), steak (page 67) or lemon pepper pork schnitzel (page 65).

**For smashed potatoes:** Pierce the potatoes all over with a fork, wrap in kitchen paper, place on a plate and microwave for 10 minutes (900W). You should be able to easily pierce them with a skewer all the way through without resistance.

Place the hot potatoes in a large bowl and add the butter, olive oil, salt and pepper. Stir well and allow the butter to melt under the heat of the potatoes for 3–4 minutes. Stir once more after the butter has melted.

Heat or preheat the air fryer to 200°C/400°F. Place the potatoes in the air fryer, ensuring there is generous space between them. Take a potato masher and squash each potato so that it is around 1cm (½ inch) thick, then spray all over with a little oil. Air fry for 15 minutes until the tops are golden, crisp and crunchy.

Serve alongside spicy bean burgers (page 96), honey mustard gammon (page 109), cauliflower steak (page 55), steak (page 67) or chicken Kyivs (page 110).

**TIP**

If making hasselback or smashed potatoes in a two-drawer air fryer, it's essential that you split them between both drawers for speed and the crispest finish. If you must use just one drawer, simply cook the full quantity in two batches.

# ULTIMATE CHEESE TOASTIE 3 WAYS

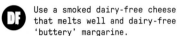

Use a smoked dairy-free cheese that melts well and dairy-free 'buttery' margarine.

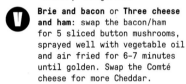

**Brie and bacon** or **Three cheese and ham**: swap the bacon/ham for 5 sliced button mushrooms, sprayed well with vegetable oil and air fried for 6-7 minutes until golden. Swap the Comté cheese for more Cheddar.

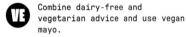

Combine dairy-free and vegetarian advice and use vegan mayo.

- 2 tsp buttery margarine
- 2 slices of gluten-free white bread
- 1½ tsp mayonnaise

**For Brie and bacon**
- 2 slices of smoked bacon
- 4 large slices of Brie

**For cheese and chive**
- 2 square slices of Emmental cheese
- 1 tsp finely chopped chives

**For three cheese and ham**
- Small handful of a mixture of grated extra-mature Cheddar, Red Leicester and Comté
- 2 slices of ham

**Serves 1 / Takes 10 minutes**

Oh how I wish I could just walk into a coffee shop and grab one of these! Fortunately for us, the air fryer results in a toastie that's super-crispy on the outside (no matter how questionable your gluten-free bread is) with lots of melted, gooey cheese, in next to no time at all. Using mayonnaise on the outside somehow almost fries the bread for a golden finish – only a thin layer is needed, or it can make bread soggy.

If making the Brie and bacon toastie, heat or preheat the air fryer to 200°C/400°F and air fry the bacon for 6–8 minutes or until it is as crispy as you like it.

Spread the margarine on both slices of bread, flip and thinly spread the mayonnaise on the other sides.

Heat or preheat the air fryer to 200°C/400°F (if you haven't done so already). Place one slice of bread in the air fryer, mayonnaise side down, and top with the cheese and either chives, air fried bacon or ham, depending on which variation you're making – be careful if your air fryer is already hot!

Place the other slice of bread on top, mayonnaise side up, gently press it down and air fry for 7–8 minutes or until the bread is crisp and browned at the edges, flipping it halfway through.

## TIP

For a loaded cheese on toast/toasted open sandwich vibe, omit the second slice of bread and reduce the cooking time by a couple of minutes. Just ensure you press your toppings onto the bread firmly to avoid them being blown about by the powerful air fryer fan.

# CAULIFLOWER 3 WAYS

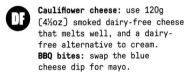

**Cauliflower cheese:** use 120g (4½oz) smoked dairy-free cheese that melts well, and a dairy-free alternative to cream.
**BBQ bites:** swap the blue cheese dip for mayo.

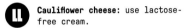

**Cauliflower cheese:** use lactose-free cream.

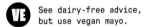

See dairy-free advice, but use vegan mayo.

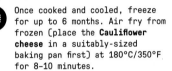

Once cooked and cooled, freeze for up to 6 months. Air fry from frozen (place the **Cauliflower cheese** in a suitably-sized baking pan first) at 180°C/350°F for 8-10 minutes.

- Vegetable oil in a spray bottle, for greasing

**For cauliflower cheese**
- 1 small cauliflower (700g/ 1lb 8½oz), cut into 5cm (2 inch) florets
- 100ml (generous ⅓ cup) double (heavy) cream
- ½ tsp each of salt and ground black pepper
- 1 tsp wholegrain mustard
- 60g (2¼oz) extra-mature Cheddar cheese, grated
- 60g (2¼oz) mozzarella, grated

**Serves 2 / Takes 25 minutes**

With the amount of bland, boiled cauliflower I've eaten in my life, I was about ready to retire from eating it entirely... until I bought my air fryer. Not only does it add a light, crispy finish, but it somehow improves the internal texture so that it melts in your mouth and bestows so much more flavour. To celebrate my new-found love of the humble cauliflower, here are three of my favourite variations that I will certainly never retire from my meal plans. For two-drawer air fryers, either split the florets between both drawers for the cauliflower cheese or BBQ bites, or cook in two separate batches if using only one of the drawers.

**For cauliflower cheese:** Place the cauliflower florets in a microwave-safe bowl, add 1 tablespoon of water and loosely cover with a plate. Microwave on full power for 7–8 minutes (900W) until cooked through. Alternatively, boil in a small saucepan for 5 minutes, then drain.

Transfer the cooked cauliflower to a large bowl, add the cream, salt and pepper, mustard and Cheddar, then mix well.

Heat or preheat the air fryer to 200°C/400°F (crisping tray or basket removed).

Add the cauliflower cheese to the air fryer and air fry for 5–6 minutes. Sprinkle the mozzarella on top and air fry for another 4–5 minutes or until the cheese is golden brown.

Serve with a roast dinner centrepiece, like my toad in the hole (page 81), whole chicken (page 56), pork steaks (page 65) or honey mustard gammon (page 109) alongside air fryer Yorkshire puddings (page 182) and lots of gluten-free gravy.

**continued overleaf**

**For crispy BBQ cauliflower bites (pictured on page 53)**

- 1 small cauliflower (700g/1lb 8½oz), cut into 2.5cm (1 inch) florets
- 2 tbsp garlic-infused oil
- 3 tbsp gluten-free plain (all-purpose) flour or cornflour (cornstarch)
- 5 tbsp gluten-free BBQ sauce
- Small handful of spring onion (scallion) greens, finely chopped
- Blue cheese dip (shop-bought), to serve (optional)

**For gunpowder cauliflower steaks**

- 1 large cauliflower (about 1kg/2lb 3oz)
- 4 tbsp garlic-infused oil
- 2½ tsp garam masala
- 1 tsp dried chilli flakes or Kashmiri chilli flakes
- 1 tsp dried fenugreek
- ½ tsp salt
- 1½ tsp gluten-free plain (all-purpose) flour or cornflour (cornstarch)
- Small handful of coriander (cilantro), finely chopped, to serve

**For crispy BBQ cauliflower bites:** Add the cauliflower florets, garlic-infused oil and flour to a large bowl, and mix to combine.

Heat or preheat the air fryer to 200°C/400°F. Generously grease the base of the air fryer basket or crisping tray by spraying it with oil.

Add the cauliflower to the air fryer basket and air fry for 15 minutes until golden brown in places, turning over and spraying with oil halfway through. Remove to a (cleaned) bowl, add the BBQ sauce and toss until well coated.

Sprinkle with the spring onion greens and optionally serve alongside a blue cheese dip or use as a fajita/taco filling alongside your usual favourite toppings.

**For gunpowder cauliflower steaks:** Slice the cauliflower using a large knife, creating two thick 'steaks', 2.5cm (1 inch) thick, from the middle of the cauliflower. Reserve the rest of the cauliflower for a future dinner or for one of the recipes above – you should have the perfect amount left over for either the cauliflower cheese or bites.

In a small dish, combine the garlic-infused oil, garam masala, chilli flakes, fenugreek, salt and flour. Brush onto the cauliflower steaks on both sides.

Heat or preheat the air fryer to 180°C/350°F. Lightly grease the base of the air fryer basket or crisping tray by spraying it with a little oil.

Add the cauliflower steaks to the air fryer basket (both should comfortably fit without touching) and air fry for 18–20 minutes, turning over and spraying with oil halfway through.

Sprinkle with chopped coriander and serve alongside air fryer chips (page 38), sweet potato cubes (page 41), 'roast' potatoes (page 44) or rice and onion rings (page 181).

# WHOLE CHICKEN 3 WAYS

**Garlic, lemon and herb:** use a dairy-free 'buttery' margarine instead of butter.

**Garlic, lemon and herb:** use garlic-infused oil instead of garlic paste. **Chinese** or **Tandoori-style:** brush with maple syrup instead of honey or mango chutney.

Once cooked and cooled, strip the chicken meat from the bones and freeze for up to 3 months. Defrost in the fridge.

- 1 medium chicken, about 1.6kg (3½lb)

**For a garlic, lemon and herb coating**
- 75g (⅓ cup) butter, melted
- 3 tsp garlic paste or 3 tbsp garlic-infused oil
- Grated zest and juice of 1 small lemon
- ½ tsp each of salt and ground black pepper
- 1½ tbsp dried mixed herbs

**For a sticky Chinese-style coating**
- 2 tbsp gluten-free soy sauce
- 2 tsp Chinese five spice powder
- 1 tbsp sesame oil
- 1 tsp ground white pepper
- 1½ tsp honey mixed with 1 tsp gluten-free soy sauce (for brushing later)

**continued overleaf**

**Serves 4 / Takes 1 hour**

**Whether you need a crispy whole chicken as the centrepiece of your roast or simply fancy the best 'roast' chicken sandwiches ever, these three mouthwatering flavour variations have got you covered. If your chicken is closer to 1.3kg (2¾lb), decrease the cooking time by 5 minutes, but I wouldn't recommend anything larger than 1.6kg (3½lb), as it's unlikely to fit in your air fryer!**

Begin preparing the chicken by optionally tying both ends of the legs together with string, which will make getting the chicken in and out of the air fryer a lot easier.

In a small bowl, mix together the ingredients for the coating of your choice (without the ingredient for brushing later), then rub half all over the top of the chicken, reserving the rest for later. If making the lemon and herb chicken, stuff the used lemon halves inside the cavity of the chicken.

Heat or preheat the air fryer to 190°C/375°F.

Place the chicken in the air fryer basket breast side down, then rub the underside all over with most of the reserved coating. Air fry for 30 minutes.

Flip the chicken, rub with the remaining coating and air fry for a further 25 minutes, brushing with either honey/soy sauce or mango chutney (if making either the Chinese or tandoori-style chicken) 5 minutes before it's done. Check the inner thigh of the chicken with a digital cooking thermometer to ensure it's done: it should read at least 74°C/165°F.

Remove from the air fryer (letting any juices from the cavity drip back into the air fryer before removing), transfer to a wooden board and allow to rest for 5–10 minutes before carving.

**continued overleaf**

**For a sticky tandoori-style coating (pictured on page 57)**

- 1 tbsp mild curry powder
- ½ tsp garam masala
- ½ tsp dried chilli flakes
- 1 tsp smoked paprika
- 1 tsp ginger paste
- 3 tbsp vegetable oil or garlic-infused oil
- ½ tsp each of salt and ground black pepper
- 1 tbsp water
- 2 tbsp mango chutney (for brushing later)

Serve with either cauliflower cheese (page 52) chips (page 38) or 'roast' potatoes (44) and roast dinner veggies. Alternatively, strip the bones of all the meat, allow to cool completely and keep the meat covered in the fridge for up to 4 days to use in future meals or sandwiches.

**TIP**

Flipping a hot whole chicken in a very hot, very confined air fryer drawer can be a little tricky! I usually just use a large meat fork (the kind you'd use to help carve a turkey) to impale the entire chicken beneath the breast and lift it out, then flip.

# CHICKEN WINGS 3 WAYS

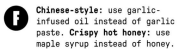

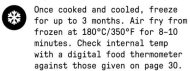

**Chinese-style:** use garlic-infused oil instead of garlic paste. **Crispy hot honey:** use maple syrup instead of honey.

Once cooked and cooled, freeze for up to 3 months. Air fry from frozen at 180°C/350°F for 8–10 minutes. Check internal temp with a digital food thermometer against those given on page 30.

- 1kg (2lb 3oz) chicken wings, halved at the joint and tips removed

**For crispy chilli-lime wings**

- 3 tbsp vegetable or olive oil
- 3 tbsp gluten-free plain (all-purpose) flour or cornflour (cornstarch)
- 1 tsp gluten-free baking powder
- 1 tsp salt
- 1 tsp dried chilli flakes
- Grated zest and juice of ½ lime, to serve

**For Chinese-style wings**

- 1 tsp garlic paste or 2 tbsp garlic-infused oil
- 2 tsp Chinese five spice powder
- 3 tbsp dark brown sugar
- 2 tsp ginger paste
- 2 tbsp gluten-free soy sauce
- Small handful of spring onion (scallion) greens, finely sliced, to serve

**continued overleaf**

---

**Serves 4 / Takes 25 minutes**

The speed at which you can churn out super-crispy wings in the air fryer is nothing more than mind-boggling, so here are my three favourite variations, each with its own unique flavour twist. To prepare the chicken wings so they're in two small pieces (a separate drumette and flat piece instead of one big wing piece), simply cut them in half at the joint with a large, sharp knife; usually the tips (the pointy part with no meat on it) are removed already, but if not, simply chop these off and discard.

Add the chicken wings to a large bowl.

**For chilli-lime wings:** Add the oil, flour, baking powder, salt and chilli flakes.

**For Chinese-style wings:** Add the garlic paste/garlic-infused oil, five spice, sugar, ginger and soy sauce.

**For hot honey wings:** Add the oil, flour, baking powder and salt; combine the honey, chilli flakes and vinegar in a small dish and set aside.

Mix well until everything is evenly dispersed and the chicken is well coated.

Heat or preheat the air fryer to 200°C/400°F.

Place as many of the prepared wings in the air fryer basket that will comfortably fit without touching. Air fry for 16–18 minutes until crisp and golden, flipping each wing over after 10 minutes. For hot honey wings, brush each wing on both sides with the honey mixture around 5 minutes before they're done.

Repeat using any remaining chicken wings that wouldn't fit in your air fryer.

**continued overleaf**

**For crispy hot honey wings**

- 3 tbsp vegetable or olive oil
- 3 tbsp gluten-free plain (all-purpose) flour or cornflour (cornstarch)
- 1 tsp gluten-free baking powder
- 1 tsp salt
- 5 tbsp honey
- 1½ tsp dried chilli flakes, plus a little extra to serve
- 3 tsp apple cider vinegar

**To serve the chilli-lime wings:** sprinkle over the lime zest and squeeze the lime juice over.

**To serve the Chinese-style wings:** sprinkle with the sliced spring onion greens.

**To serve the hot honey wings:** sprinkle with a little more chilli flakes.

Serve as a main alongside chips or wedges (page 38), mashed potato, sweet potato fries, cubes or fritters (page 41) or alongside Chinese fakeaway favourites such as my Singapore stir fry (page 129) or egg-fried rice (page 165).

## TIP

If using a two-drawer air fryer, you'll most definitely need to employ both drawers to ensure that the chicken wings have adequate space between them for speed and the crispest finish. If you have to use just one drawer, simply cook the full quantity in two batches.

# SALMON 3 WAYS

 **Teriyaki** or **Honey mustard:** use maple syrup instead of honey.

 Once cooked and cooled, freeze for up to 3 months. Air fry from frozen at 180°C/350°F for 7-8 minutes. Check internal temp with a digital food thermometer against those given on page 30.

- 2 salmon fillets, skin on (260g/9¼oz in total)
- Vegetable oil in a spray bottle, for greasing

**For teriyaki salmon**
- 2 tbsp gluten-free soy sauce
- 1 tsp mirin or rice wine vinegar
- 1 tsp ginger paste
- 1 tbsp garlic-infused oil
- 1 tsp cornflour (cornstarch)
- 2 tbsp honey, for brushing

**For Cajun salmon (pictured)**
- 1 tbsp garlic-infused oil
- 1 tsp smoked paprika
- ½ tsp chilli powder
- Pinch of ground coriander
- Pinch of ground allspice
- Pinch of ground ginger

**For honey mustard salmon**
- 1 tsp wholegrain mustard
- 2 tsp honey

**Serves 2 / Takes 15 minutes**

**A quick 10-minute blast in the air fryer is all it takes to cook melt-in-the-mouth salmon with a seriously crispy skin. With either a teriyaki, Cajun or honey mustard finish, these three variations only require a few store-cupboard ingredients and never fail to add a tidal wave of flavour.**

Pat the salmon dry on all sides with kitchen paper. In a small dish, mix together the ingredients for the coating of your choice (omitting the honey for brushing in the teriyaki version) and set aside.

Heat or preheat the air fryer to 200°C/400°F.

Generously grease the base of the air fryer basket or crisping tray by spraying it with oil – salmon is quite prone to sticking to the base of the crisping drawer, so ensure you grease it well.

Brush the tops and sides of each salmon fillet with some coating, then place skin side up in the air fryer. Brush the skin with the rest of your coating and air fry for 9–10 minutes, flipping them 3 minutes before they're done. If making teriyaki salmon, ensure you brush each side with honey before and after flipping. The salmon skin should be crisp and a little charred at the edges.

Serve with egg-fried rice (page 165), mashed potato, air fryer wedges (page 38), smashed potatoes (page 47) and air fried veggies of your choice (page 175).

# PORK STEAK 3 WAYS

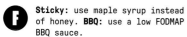

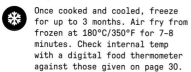

**Sticky:** use maple syrup instead of honey. **BBQ:** use a low FODMAP BBQ sauce.

Once cooked and cooled, freeze for up to 3 months. Air fry from frozen at 180°C/350°F for 7–8 minutes. Check internal temp with a digital food thermometer against those given on page 30.

- 4 boneless pork loin steaks (400g/14oz each) or pork chops (700g/1lb 8½oz each), bone removed
- Vegetable oil in a spray bottle, for greasing

## For sticky pork steaks

- 2 tbsp orange juice
- 1 tsp Tabasco
- 1 tbsp black treacle
- 1 tbsp honey
- 1 tbsp Dijon mustard
- ½ tsp salt

## For lemon pepper pork schnitzel (pictured)

- 6 tbsp gluten-free plain (all-purpose) flour or cornflour (cornstarch)
- ½ tsp salt
- 1 large egg
- 100g (generous 1½ cups) gluten-free breadcrumbs
- Grated zest of 1 large lemon
- ½ tsp coarsely ground black pepper

## For BBQ pork steaks

- ½ tbsp smoked paprika
- 1½ tbsp light brown sugar
- ½ tsp salt
- 4 tbsp gluten-free BBQ sauce

**Serves 4 / Takes 15–20 minutes**

It couldn't be easier to transform pork loin steaks or pork chops (see the TIPS overleaf for the difference between them!) into the glorious centrepiece of many future family favourites to come. Either choose my sticky pork steaks (which are mildly spicy, sweet and bold), lemon pepper pork schnitzel (dedicated to my editor Harriet!), which are coated in crispy, golden breadcrumbs, or my classic smoky BBQ pork steaks.

**For sticky pork steaks:** Mix together the coating ingredients in a small dish. Brush both sides of the pork steaks until evenly coated. Optionally cover and chill in the fridge for 15 minutes and up to 12 hours.

**For lemon pepper pork schnitzel:** Place the pork steaks on a chopping board and cover with cling film (plastic wrap). Using a rolling pin or meat mallet, gently bash until 5mm (¼ inch) thick.

Spread the flour out on a large dinner plate and mix in the salt. In a medium bowl, briefly beat the egg with a fork. Grab another large dinner plate and spread out the breadcrumbs, lemon zest and black pepper, mixing them briefly together.

Dredge one flattened pork steak on the flour plate until evenly dusted on both sides, then dip into the egg bowl until well coated. Finally, dredge in the breadcrumbs, ensuring even coverage on both sides, gently pressing and compacting them onto the steaks. Repeat with the rest of the pork steaks.

**For BBQ pork steaks:** Mix together the smoked paprika, sugar and salt in a small dish. Rub onto each pork steak until evenly coated.

Heat or preheat the air fryer to 180°C/350°F.

Generously grease the base of the air fryer basket or crisping tray by spraying it with oil.

**continued overleaf**

Place the prepared pork steaks in the air fryer and lightly spray with oil. Air fry for 8–9 minutes, flipping them halfway through and following one of the three instructions below, depending on the variation you're making:

**If making sticky pork steaks:** brush each side with more of the sticky marinade before and after flipping.

**If making lemon pepper pork schnitzel:** spray both sides generously with oil before and after flipping.

**If making BBQ pork steaks:** generously brush each side with BBQ sauce before and after flipping.

If making the sticky or BBQ versions, leave to rest for 5 minutes (skip this for schnitzel, so the breadcrumbs stay crisp), then serve with mashed potato, air fryer chips (page 38), smashed potatoes (page 47) or hot honey sweet potato cubes (page 41) and the veggies of your choice.

## TIPS

Pork loin steaks are essentially pork chops with the bone already removed, so buy these if you can, to save time; otherwise you'll have to remove the bone yourself.

As pork loin steaks/pork chops are usually quite thin cuts already, they're incredibly easy to overcook and will become dry and chewy. Follow the timings above to ensure you hit the sweet spot or, to be extra sure, use a digital food thermometer to check the internal temperature when they're nearly done – it should read 63°C/145°F – and make sure you rest them.

# STEAK 3 WAYS

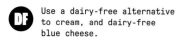 Use a dairy-free alternative to cream, and dairy-free blue cheese.

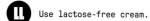 Use lactose-free cream.

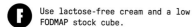 Use lactose-free cream and a low FODMAP stock cube.

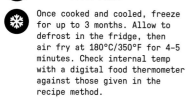 Once cooked and cooled, freeze for up to 3 months. Allow to defrost in the fridge, then air fry at 180°C/350°F for 4-5 minutes. Check internal temp with a digital food thermometer against those given in the recipe method.

- Vegetable oil in a spray bottle, for greasing
- 2 x 250g (9oz) sirloin steaks, around 2cm (¾ inch) thick
- Pinch each of salt and ground black pepper

**For a peppercorn sauce**

- 150ml (⅝ cup) gluten-free beef stock
- 125ml (½ cup) double (heavy) cream
- 2½ tsp coarsely ground black pepper
- 1 tsp gluten-free plain (all-purpose) flour or cornflour (cornstarch) mixed with 3 tsp water, to thicken the sauce

**For a blue cheese sauce**

- 100ml (generous ⅓ cup) gluten-free beef stock
- 175ml (¾ cup) double (heavy) cream
- 50g (1¾oz) blue cheese, crumbled (I use Stilton)

**For a creamy mustard sauce**

- 100ml (generous ⅓ cup) gluten-free beef stock
- 175ml (¾ cup) double (heavy) cream
- 2 tbsp wholegrain mustard

**Serves 2 / Takes 25 minutes**

**The ultimate steak night is just five ingredients away, starring a stupendously succulent steak cooked to your liking, and your choice of either peppercorn, blue cheese or creamy mustard sauce. As timings for a rare, medium or well-done steak are very precise, I've included TIPS overleaf on a few things to consider, though my biggest tip would be this: get a digital food thermometer if you intend to cook a lot of steak (and meat/fish in general) in your air fryer! I've included the internal temperatures below too for those who have one.**

Heat or preheat the air fryer to 200°C/400°F.

Lightly grease the base of the air fryer basket or crisping tray by spraying it with a little oil.

Season the steaks on both sides with salt and pepper, then place both in the air fryer – as long as they comfortably fit with around a 5cm (2 inch) space between each; if not, air fry them separately. Lightly spray with oil and follow the timings below, depending on how you prefer your steak to be cooked:

- **For rare:** air fry for 7–9 minutes, flipping halfway (45–50°C/113–122°F internal temperature)

- **For medium:** air fry for 10–12 minutes, flipping halfway (60–65°C/140–149°F internal temperature)

- **For well-done:** air fry for 13–15 minutes, flipping halfway (70–75°C/158–167°F internal temperature)

Be sure to note the TIPS overleaf for some of the factors that can greatly affect cooking time! Allow the steaks to rest for 10 minutes. Meanwhile, prepare the sauce of your choice.

Add the beef stock to a small saucepan over a medium-high heat and, as soon as it starts to rapidly bubble, add the cream and black pepper **OR** blue cheese **OR** mustard and continue to heat until it starts to gently bubble, then immediately turn the heat down to low–medium. Simmer for 5 minutes or until the sauce thickens slightly.

**continued overleaf**

**In the case of the peppercorn sauce**, the pepper turns the sauce that distinctive light brown colour but the peppercorn sauce will not thicken at this stage. Once it is brown, pour in the flour slurry while stirring quickly, and simmer for 2–3 more minutes until thickened to your liking.

Serve the steaks with your chosen sauce, alongside French fries (page 38) or smashed potatoes (page 47) and onion rings (page 181) and air fried veggies of your choice (page 175).

## TIPS

Cramming 2 steaks into a small air fryer drawer will greatly increase the timings given on the previous page – it's important that a good amount of hot air is able to circulate through the holes of the crisping tray or air fryer basket. If you have two drawers, use both.

If your air fryer doesn't need to preheat and you are air frying the steaks individually, bear in mind that the second steak will cook faster as the drawer will now be fully heated.

If your steaks are closer to room temperature and not straight out of the fridge, allow the air fryer 3–4 minutes to preheat with nothing in it first, as room-temperature steaks will cook faster than the given timings.

If your steaks are thicker or thinner than specified, adjust your timing expectations accordingly.

# WEEKNIGHT FAVOURITES

Welcome to the chapter that, in harmony with the Essentials chapter, will see you easily able to prepare an entire dinner in the air fryer.

So often, the air fryer is used to cook a piece of plain or unambitiously seasoned protein and… most probably chips, which, while still great, also greatly limits the possibilities on your plate.

And that's why this chapter is dedicated to pure variety, with dishes that are not only speedy or incredibly low effort, but will fill in all the gaps in your meal plans that might otherwise end up being filled with something bland and boring.

So be prepared to discover how to whip up everything from a pasta bake, to toad in the hole, fish cakes, falafel, balti pie and calzone.

# SWEET POTATO AND RED PEPPER SOUP

 Once cooked and cooled, freeze for up to 3 months. Reheat from frozen in the microwave at 360W, breaking up chunks and stirring every 3-4 minutes until piping hot. Freeze croûtons separately and air fry at 180°C/350°F for 4-5 minutes until crisp.

- 1 small sweet potato (325g/11½oz unpeeled weight), peeled and chopped into 1cm (½ inch) chunks
- 2 red (bell) peppers, deseeded and chopped into 2.5cm (1 inch) chunks
- 2 tbsp garlic-infused oil
- 1 tsp garam masala
- 650ml (2¾ cups) gluten-free vegetable stock
- 50g (1¾oz) leek, finely chopped
- Salt and ground black pepper
- Small handful of coriander (cilantro), roughly chopped, to serve

**For the croûtons**
- 2 small gluten-free ciabatta rolls, chopped into large, 2.5cm (1 inch) cubes
- 3 tbsp garlic-infused oil
- ½ tbsp dried mixed herbs

**Serves 2-3 / Takes 25 minutes**

This recipe exists not only because this budget-friendly starter, lunch or lazy dinner is too delicious not to share, but also because it's an excuse to showcase how to 'roast' veg and create quick gluten-free croûtons in an air fryer. Not only do both of these tasks take far less time than they would in the oven, but you could also incorporate the roasted veggies as a side alongside other meals, or enjoy the croûtons in a salad. Of course, this soup is legendary as a whole too, so ensure you add this to your meal plans ASAP!

Add the chopped sweet potato and red pepper to a large bowl. Add the garlic-infused oil, garam masala and ¼ teaspoon each of salt and pepper, then stir well until everything is well coated.

Heat or preheat the air fryer to 180°C/350°F.

Transfer the veg to the air fryer (crisping tray or basket in) and spread out into an even, flat layer. Air fry for 16–18 minutes, turning everything over halfway through, or until everything is a little blackened at the edges and nicely softened.

Meanwhile, bring the vegetable stock to the boil in a pan on the stove, add the leek and simmer for 5 minutes.

Prepare the croûtons by adding the ingredients to the empty veg bowl with a pinch each of salt and pepper. Stir to coat the ciabatta cubes.

Once the veggies are done, add them to the stock, then place the croûtons in the air fryer for 6–7 minutes, turning them over halfway through, or until golden and crisp.

Use a stick blender to blend the soup until smooth, adding more stock if needed to achieve your desired thickness. Serve topped with coriander and the croûtons.

# CHICKEN AND BACON PASTA BAKE

 Use dairy-free cream cheese and a smoked dairy-free cheese instead of Cheddar.

 Use lactose-free cream cheese.

 See low lactose advice.

 Swap the chicken for 1 large red (bell) pepper, deseeded and chopped into 1.5cm (⅝ inch) chunks, and the bacon for 100g (3½oz) broccoli florets.

 Combine dairy-free and vegetarian advice.

 Once cooked and cooled, freeze for up to 3 months. Air fry from frozen at 180°C/350°F for 6-7 minutes until piping hot.

- 200g (7oz) dried gluten-free penne
- 250g (9oz) skinless chicken breast fillets, chopped into 1.5cm (⅝ inch) bite-sized chunks
- 3 slices of smoked bacon, cut into 1cm (½ inch) strips
- 130g (generous ½ cup) cream cheese
- 60g (2¼oz) extra-mature Cheddar, grated
- 2 tbsp garlic-infused oil (optional)
- ½ tsp each of salt and ground black pepper
- 3 tbsp gluten-free breadcrumbs
- Small handful of parsley, finely chopped (optional)

**Serves 2 / Takes 20 minutes**

**Inspired by a brisk walk past all of the ready meals I can't eat in the supermarket, I've had a craving for creamy, cheesy pasta packed with tender chicken and crispy, smoky bacon ever since. With a proper 'al forno'-style finish on the cheesy, crunchy breadcrumbs on top, this dish is the ultimate definition of quick, easy and speedy comfort food.**

Heat or preheat the air fryer to 200°C/400°F.

Cook the dried pasta in a pan of salted boiling water, according to the packet instructions, until al dente, then drain.

Meanwhile, add the chopped chicken and bacon to the air fryer (basket or crisping tray in) and spread out into an even, flat layer. Air fry for 10 minutes, shaking the drawer or turning everything over halfway through, until the bacon has turned a little crispy and golden at the edges.

Add the drained pasta to the chicken and bacon in the air fryer, along with the cream cheese, half the Cheddar, the garlic-infused oil, if using, and some salt and pepper. Allow to rest for 2–3 minutes until the cream cheese has softened, then stir in until there are no lumps of cheese.

Spread everything out into an even layer and top with the rest of the Cheddar, then sprinkle over the breadcrumbs. Air fry for a final 5 minutes until the top is golden and crisp.

Sprinkle with chopped parsley and serve alongside some rocket (arugula) and gluten-free garlic bread (page 192).

## TIP

If your air fryer has space, feel free to add 1 large red (bell) pepper, deseeded and chopped into 1.5cm (⅔ inch) chunks, along with the chicken and bacon.

# 15-MINUTE PESTO AND PEA GNOCCHI

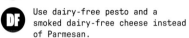 Use dairy-free pesto and a smoked dairy-free cheese instead of Parmesan.

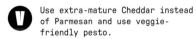 Use extra-mature Cheddar instead of Parmesan and use veggie-friendly pesto.

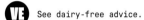 See dairy-free advice.

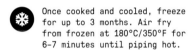 Once cooked and cooled, freeze for up to 3 months. Air fry from frozen at 180°C/350°F for 6-7 minutes until piping hot.

- Vegetable oil in a spray bottle, for greasing
- 500g (1lb 2oz) fresh gluten-free gnocchi
- 3 tbsp green pesto
- 50g (1¾oz) Parmesan, finely grated
- 150g (5½oz) sun-dried tomatoes, roughly chopped, plus 2 tbsp oil from the jar
- ¼ tsp each of salt and ground black pepper
- 100g (3½oz) frozen peas
- 4 tbsp pine nuts

**Serves 2 / Takes 15 minutes**

If ever there was a meal that everyone would think you slaved over for hours to prepare, it's this! In reality, I came up with this dish when I had very little in my fridge apart from gnocchi and cheese, so I raided my cupboards (and the freezer) for the rest... and this was the triumphant result. Coated in creamy, cheesy pesto with sun-dried tomatoes, peas and crunchy toasted pine nuts, it's hard to believe you can make this gnocchi in 15 minutes using just six ingredients and a little oil, salt and pepper.

Heat or preheat the air fryer to 200°C/400°F.

Lightly grease the base of the air fryer basket or crisping tray by spraying it with a little oil. Add the gnocchi in an even layer, generously spray with oil and air fry for 8 minutes until the gnocchi is a little golden, turning them halfway through.

Meanwhile, combine the pesto, Parmesan, sun-dried tomatoes, sun-dried tomato oil, salt and pepper in a small dish.

Add the pesto mixture and frozen peas to the gnocchi in the air fryer and turn everything over a few times until the gnocchi are well coated. Air fry for 4 minutes, turn everything over once more, then scatter the pine nuts on top and air fry for a final 3 minutes or until the pine nuts are lightly golden brown.

Optionally serve scattered with fresh basil and rocket (arugula) and with gluten-free garlic bread (page 192) on the side.

### TIP

You can find a recipe for homemade gnocchi in my first book, *How to Make Anything Gluten Free.* The supermarket gluten-free gnocchi I use is fresh and stored in the chillers along with all the other gluten-containing pasta. You can often find ambient gluten-free gnocchi in the free-from aisle too – the ambient version isn't 'fresh' so you'll need to prepare it according to the packet instructions before using it in this recipe.

# TOMATO, PEPPER AND FETA PASTA

DF Use a dairy-free feta alternative.

VE See dairy-free advice.

Once cooked and cooled, freeze for up to 3 months. Air fry from frozen at 180°C/350°F for 7-8 minutes until piping hot.

- 1 yellow (bell) pepper, deseeded and cut into 1cm (½ inch) chunks
- 5 tbsp garlic-infused oil or olive oil
- 200g (7oz) dried gluten-free pasta
- 450g (1lb) cherry tomatoes
- 150g (5½oz) feta
- ½ tsp each of salt and ground black pepper
- Handful of basil leaves, roughly chopped, plus extra to serve

**Serves 2–3 / Takes 35 minutes**

**Meet my version of the Internet's favourite viral pasta recipe, air fryer style. If you're wondering what all the fuss is about, it's simple: with a rich tomato sauce composed of 'roasted' tomatoes and fresh basil, blended with smooth, creamy and flavourful feta cheese, it's hard to believe you made it yourself using so few ingredients. Trust me, you just need to try it!**

Heat or preheat the air fryer to 200°C/400°F (crisping tray or basket removed).

Add the yellow pepper and oil to the air fryer and shake/stir well until the pepper is coated. Air fry for 10 minutes until the pepper is softened.

Meanwhile, cook the pasta in a pan of boiling salted water according to the packet instructions, until al dente, then drain.

Add the cherry tomatoes and the whole block of feta to the air fryer with the peppers and shake/stir well once more until the tomatoes are well coated in the oil. Air fry for 20 minutes, turning the tomatoes over halfway through, then add the salt, pepper and basil. Stir well until it forms a wonderful, thick and creamy tomato sauce.

Add the drained pasta and stir it in until well coated in the sauce. Air fry for a further 2–3 minutes until the sauce has reduced a little.

Sprinkle with extra chopped basil and serve with gluten-free garlic bread (page 192).

# TOAD IN THE HOLE

 Use dairy-free milk.

 Use lactose-free milk.

 Use lactose-free milk and FODMAP-friendly sausages.

 Use gluten-free and veggie-friendly sausages.

 Once cooked and cooled, freeze for up to 3 months. Air fry from frozen at 180°C/350°F for 10 minutes. Check internal temp of the sausages with a digital food thermometer against those given on page 30.

- 2 tsp vegetable oil
- 6 gluten-free pork sausages
- 2 large eggs
- 70g (generous ½ cup) cornflour (cornstarch)
- 100ml (generous ⅓ cup) milk

**Serves 2 / Takes 30 minutes**

**For this air fryer version of an English classic, you'll either need two foil containers (the kind you'd expect to see takeaway food delivered in) or two silicone air fryer liners that will fit in your air fryer to support the wet batter as it cooks. Mine are 15 x 20cm (6 x 8 inches) and each container is suitably sized for one individual toad in the hole – but as long as the container fits into your air fryer, that's the important part!**

Heat or preheat the air fryer to 180°C/350°F.

Place a teaspoon of oil in each of the two foil containers or silicone air fryer liners (see measurements above) and add 3 sausages per container. Place the containers in the air fryer for about 5–7 minutes until the sausages are starting to colour, turning them over halfway through.

Meanwhile, make the batter by mixing the eggs and cornflour together in a medium bowl until combined, then gradually whisk in the milk a third at a time.

Pour half of the batter into each container, which should be super-hot and sizzle as you pour it in. Continue to air fry for 15–17 minutes until risen and golden brown – try not to open the air fryer until at least 12 minutes have passed. When done, the sausages should be browned and the batter should be super puffy and crisp.

Serve alongside air fryer roast potatoes (page 44), air fried veggies (page 175) and lots of gluten-free gravy.

## TIP

If your foil container or air fryer liner is considerably smaller than mine (see recipe intro) then the batter will struggle to rise as much when cooked and will become stodgy – in this case, use less mixture per container. If your container is considerably larger than mine, you might find it cooks even faster than the timings given, so keep an eye on it.

# CRISPY PARMESAN CHICKEN

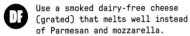
Use a smoked dairy-free cheese (grated) that melts well instead of Parmesan and mozzarella.

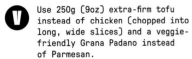
Use 250g (9oz) extra-firm tofu instead of chicken (chopped into long, wide slices) and a veggie-friendly Grana Padano instead of Parmesan.

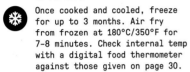
Once cooked and cooled, freeze for up to 3 months. Air fry from frozen at 180°C/350°F for 7-8 minutes. Check internal temp with a digital food thermometer against those given on page 30.

- 2 skinless chicken breast fillets
- 3 tbsp gluten-free plain (all-purpose) flour or cornflour (cornstarch)
- 1 tsp salt
- ½ tsp ground black or white pepper
- 1 large egg
- 50g (scant 1 cup) gluten-free breadcrumbs
- 40g (1½oz) Parmesan, grated, plus extra to finish
- Vegetable oil in a spray bottle, for greasing
- ½ x 125g (4½oz) ball of mozzarella, thinly sliced
- 5-6 basil leaves, roughly chopped

**For the sauce**
- 1 tsp garlic-infused oil
- 100ml (generous ⅓ cup) tomato passata
- 1 tsp dried mixed herbs

**Serves 2 / Takes 25 minutes**

**Think tender chicken, coated with cheesy breadcrumbs, topped with my easy-peasy pizza sauce and lots of golden brown, stringy mozzarella. Crisping up those breadcrumbs has never been easier than in an air fryer, and achieving that pizza-oven-like finish on the tomato sauce and mozzarella is guaranteed.**

To prepare the chicken breasts, butterfly them carefully using a sharp knife: lay them flat and slice horizontally so you can open each like a book, being careful not to cut all the way through! If you're not familiar with this technique (you could search online), you can always place the chicken breasts between 2 sheets of cling film (plastic wrap) and bash until flat with a rolling pin or meat mallet. Either way, we're aiming to make the chicken as flat as possible so it'll get more of that crispy coating and cook twice as fast.

Spread the flour, salt and pepper out on a large dinner plate, ensuring everything is nicely mixed. Briefly beat the egg with a fork in a medium bowl. Grab another large dinner plate and spread out the breadcrumbs and Parmesan, then briefly mix together.

Dredge the prepared chicken in the flour until evenly dusted on both sides, then dip into the egg bowl until well coated. Finally, dredge in the cheesy breadcrumbs, ensuring even coverage on both sides, gently squeezing and compacting them to the chicken.

Heat or preheat the air fryer to 200°C/400°F.

Lightly grease the base of the air fryer basket or crisping tray by spraying it with a little oil.

Place the prepared chicken in the air fryer basket and spray with oil, making sure they're both touching as little as possible (or place in separate air fryer drawers). Air fry for 8 minutes until the breadcrumbs are starting to turn crisp and golden, turning the chicken over halfway through and spraying with oil once more.

**continued overleaf**

Meanwhile, mix the ingredients for the sauce together in a small bowl, with a pinch of salt and pepper to taste.

Top each chicken breast with dollops of the tomato sauce, followed by slices of mozzarella and some chopped basil. Air fry for another 6 minutes or until the cheese is golden brown in places.

Serve with gluten-free pasta, mashed potatoes or air fryer chips (page 38) and air fried veggies (page 175) or a side salad.

## TIP

Save any leftover passata for my air fryer pizzas (page 144), chicken balti pot pies (page 147), or calzone (page 100), or use in place of chopped tomatoes in your favourite pasta dishes.

# PROPER FISH CAKES

 Once cooked and cooled, freeze for up to 3 months. Air fry from frozen at 180°C/350°F for 10 minutes. Check internal temp with a digital food thermometer against those given on page 30.

- Vegetable oil in a spray bottle, for greasing
- 2 salmon or white fish fillets, skin on (260g/9¼oz in total)
- 1 large potato (about 300g/10½oz)
- 1 tbsp garlic-infused oil
- Grated zest of 1 small lemon
- Small handful of parsley, roughly chopped
- 2 tbsp gluten-free plain (all-purpose) flour
- ½ tsp each of salt and ground black pepper

**To coat the fish cakes**
- 3 tbsp gluten-free plain (all-purpose) flour
- 1 egg
- 85g (1¼ cups) gluten-free breadcrumbs

**Serves 2–3 (makes 6) / Takes 30 minutes**

**Though most of us gluten-free folks spend 99% of our time raving about where to find edible fish and chips, I'm sure you'll all agree that a proper, crispy-on-the-outside gluten-free fish cake is an underrated joy. Especially as you can make these either with salmon or white fish and it's so much healthier than if deep-frying fish cakes. I have no doubt that this recipe will keep you happy for many years to come.**

**This recipe also works really well with frozen fish. Simply measure out 260g (9¼oz) of frozen fish fillets and air fry following the temperature and timing given in the first step of the method (you'll likely need to give the frozen fish an extra 2 minutes or so in the air fryer). Also, try using 100g (3½oz) of crushed gluten-free cornflakes instead of breadcrumbs to give your fishcakes a super crisp, crunchy coating – perfect if you struggle to find gluten-free breadcrumbs in your local supermarket!**

To prepare the fish, heat or preheat the air fryer to 200°C/400°F. Lightly grease the base of the air fryer basket or crisping tray by spraying it with a little oil. Add the fish (skin side up) and air fry for 10 minutes or until the skin is crisp.

Meanwhile, pierce the potato multiple times all over and wrap in kitchen paper. Microwave for 8–10 minutes on full power (900W) until you can easily poke a sharp knife right through it. Allow to cool a little, then remove the skin and transfer the flesh to a large bowl. Alternatively, to cook the potato on the hob, peel and chop into 2cm (¾ inch) cubes, transfer to a saucepan of boiling water and simmer for 15 minutes until cooked through, then drain and transfer to a large bowl.

Once the fish is done, add it to the potato in the bowl, followed by the garlic-infused oil, lemon zest, parsley, flour, salt and pepper. Mix everything until well combined, then divide the mixture into 6 equal portions and roll into balls – around 80g (2¾oz) each.

**continued overleaf**

Spread the flour for coating over a dinner plate, beat the egg in a small bowl, then spread the breadcrumbs out on a second dinner plate.

Gently squash the balls to form patties around 2cm (¾ inch) high and roll around on the flour plate until lightly dusted on all sides. Next, coat well in beaten egg, then roll around on the breadcrumbs plate until tightly coated.

Heat or preheat the air fryer to 200°C/400°F (no need to clean it) and spray it with a little oil if there isn't much left after cooking the fish. Place as many fish cakes as will comfortably fit in the air fryer without touching, spray generously with oil then air fry for 9–10 minutes, flipping them over halfway through, until the breadcrumbs are golden and crisp.

Serve with either sweet chilli or tartare sauce, alongside sweet potato wedges, cubes or fritters (page 41) cauliflower bites (page 52), spicy potato wedges (page 38) and/or air fried veggies (page 175) and rocket (arugula).

## TIPS

Did you know you can easily give these fishcakes a melting middle? Simply chop a 125g (4½oz) ball of mozzarella into 1.5cm (⅔ inch) cubes. Once you've divided the fish cake mixture into balls, push a piece of mozzarella into the centre of each ball and re-roll them. Follow the rest of the recipe as normal and enjoy a gooey centre!

Though I've chosen to keep my fishcakes classic, you can always spice things up with... spices! Simply add either 1 tbsp of smoked paprika, curry powder, garam masala or dried mixed herbs. If you're feeling even more adventurous, try mixing 50g (1¾oz) of grated Parmesan with the breadcrumbs before coating the fishcakes to get a cheesy, golden crust on the outside. The possibilities are endless!

# LEMON PEPPER SALMON BURGERS

 Once cooked and cooled, freeze for up to 3 months. Air fry from frozen at 180°C/350°F for 8-10 minutes. Check internal temp with a digital food thermometer against those given on page 30.

- 2 salmon fillets, skin on (260g/9¼oz total), chopped into 1cm (½ inch) cubes
- ½ medium courgette (zucchini), cut into 5mm (¼ inch) cubes
- Handful of spring onion (scallion) greens, finely sliced
- 1 tbsp gluten-free soy sauce
- Grated zest of 1 lemon and juice of ½
- ½ tsp each of salt and ground black pepper
- 70g (generous ½ cup) gluten-free plain (all-purpose) flour
- 1 medium egg
- Vegetable oil in a spray bottle, for greasing

### To serve
- 3 gluten-free burger buns, split
- 3 tsp tartare sauce
- Small handful of watercress
- 3 ribboned slices of dill pickles

**Serves 3 / Takes 20 minutes**

**It's hard to believe that these chunky, zesty, peppery salmon burgers can be thrown together so quickly and air fried to perfection in 20 minutes. You could even speed up the prep time by throwing everything into a food processor and blitzing until combined yet chunky to make this the speediest, tastiest dinner on Earth!**

Place the salmon, courgette, spring onion greens, soy sauce, lemon zest and juice, salt, pepper, flour and egg in a medium bowl. Use a wooden spoon to mix together until everything is evenly combined and comes together (mix in 2–4 tablespoons more flour if needed to bring the mixture together – the amount depends on how wet the mixture is once combined).

Divide the mixture into 3 patties about 10cm (4 inches) in diameter and 1cm (½ inch) thick – use lightly floured hands or a burger press. Make sure the mixture is nicely but gently compressed together, which is key to it binding together well.

Heat or preheat the air fryer to 200°C/400°F. Lightly grease the base of the air fryer basket or crisping tray by spraying it with a little oil.

Place as many burgers in the air fryer as will comfortably fit without touching, then lightly spray with oil. Air fry for 12 minutes, flipping them after 8–9 minutes and lightly spraying with oil once again.

Lightly toast the buns in the air fryer for 2–3 minutes until the bottoms and tops are a little crisp, but the bread inside still feels squidgy.

To construct, spread a thin layer of tartare sauce on the base of each bun, then top with the watercress. Place a salmon burger on next and add a dill pickle. Spread a thin layer of tartare sauce on the cut side of the top bun, and place on top. Serve alongside air fryer chips, fries or wedges (page 38), sweet potato chips or hot honey sweet potato cubes (page 41), smashed or hasselback potatoes (page 47).

# LASAGNE

 Use a dairy-free cheese that melts well instead of mozzarella.

 Skip the steps to cook the minced (ground) beef and simply add 2 x 400g (14oz) cans of brown lentils (drained) to the passata, then follow the rest of the recipe.

 Combine the dairy-free and veggie advice.

 Once cooked and cooled, freeze for up to 3 months. Air fry from frozen at 180°C/350°F for 10–12 minutes or until piping hot in the middle.

- 500g (1lb 2oz) lean minced (ground) beef (5% fat)
- ½ tsp each of salt and ground black pepper
- 500g (1lb 2oz) passata
- 1 tbsp tomato purée (paste)
- 1 tbsp garlic-infused oil, plus a glug extra for the lasagne sheets
- 1 tbsp dried mixed herbs
- 40g (1½oz) leek or ½ small onion, finely diced
- 4-6 dried gluten-free lasagne sheets
- 200g (7oz) mozzarella, grated

**Serves 3-4 / Takes 45 minutes**

**If you didn't think you could make a lasagne in an air fryer, then think again! My version is three times quicker to make than your average lasagne recipe, yet the results are nothing short of mind-blowing. The secret here is that every single layer gets a blast of that signature air fried magic – you'll have to just try it yourself to see what I mean! Don't forget to check the TIP overleaf, as the size of your air fryer drawer will determine how many lasagne sheets you'll need and potentially how fast it'll take to cook.**

Heat or preheat the air fryer to 180°C/350°F (crisping tray or basket removed).

Add the minced beef to the air fryer, season with the salt and pepper and break it up using a wooden spoon. Air fry for 5–6 minutes, turning the beef over halfway through, until just browned.

Add the passata, tomato purée, garlic-infused oil and dried mixed herbs. Stir well, then add either the leek or onion – if using leek, stir it in; if using onion, scatter it on top in an even layer (don't stir it in yet) – and air fry for a further 15 minutes, stirring well halfway through.

Meanwhile, bring a large saucepan of water to the boil, then add a glug of oil – this should help prevent the lasagne sheets from sticking together. Add the lasagne to the boiling water and boil for 8–10 minutes until flexible and al dente.

Remove half of the ragu to a medium bowl and spread out the remaining half in the air fryer. Top with half of the cooked lasagne sheets, overlapping as little as possible, and top with half of the grated mozzarella. Air fry for 10 minutes, then add the rest of the ragu to the air fryer in an even layer.

Layer on the last lasagne sheets and the last of the mozzarella. Air fry for 5 minutes or until the top is golden brown and a little crisp. Serve with a side salad.

**continued overleaf**

## TIP

The size of your air fryer can greatly affect the cooking speed of this recipe, as well as how many lasagne sheets you'll need. I made this in one 4.5 litre (5 quart), 15 x 20cm (6 x 8 inch) air fryer drawer and used 4 lasagne sheets in total. However, if your air fryer drawer is much wider (the depth of the drawer doesn't really matter here) and your ingredients are more spread out, the beef and ragu will cook around 20% faster. Of course, if everything is more spread out too, you'll definitely need more lasagne sheets to cover it – which is why I've specified requiring up to 6 lasagne sheets in the recipe.

# MARK'S CHICKEN OR BEEF SATAY SKEWERS

 Once cooked and cooled, freeze for up to 3 months. Air fry from frozen at 180°C/350°F for 5-6 minutes. Check internal temp with a digital food thermometer against those given on page 30.

- 350g (12½oz) skinless, boneless chicken thighs, chopped into long strips 2cm (¾ inch) wide, or beef sirloin steak, any tough parts removed, chopped into 2cm (¾ inch) cubes
- Vegetable oil in a spray bottle, for greasing
- ½ cucumber, peeled into ribbons, to serve

**For the marinade**
- 1 tbsp garlic-infused oil
- 1 tsp lemongrass paste
- 2 tsp galangal or ginger paste
- 1 tsp ground turmeric
- ½ tsp ground coriander
- ½ tsp smoked paprika
- ½ tsp dried chilli flakes
- 2 tsp palm sugar or light brown sugar
- ¼ tsp salt

**Serves 2-3 / Takes 20 minutes + marinating**

**Without question, this has always been Mark's favourite street food whenever visiting his family in Malaysia. His recipe is deceptively simple: bung all the marinade ingredients in a bowl to marinate the meat, then chuck all the dipping sauce ingredients into a saucepan and simmer. The air fryer does the rest of the hard work, achieving a BBQ-like finish! You'll easily find lemongrass, galangal or ginger and tamarind paste in small jars (or squeezy tubes) alongside all the spices in supermarkets.**

Add all the ingredients for the marinade to a medium bowl and mix until well combined. Add the chicken strips or beef cubes and stir until well coated.

Cover the bowl and place in the fridge for 15 minutes and up to 12 hours.

Grab 6 wooden or metal skewers – most importantly, they need to fit into your air fryer, so check that they do first. Wooden skewers can be trimmed to fit.

Thread the chicken strips or beef cubes evenly onto 6 skewers.

Heat or preheat the air fryer to 200°C/400°F. Lightly grease the base of the air fryer basket or crisping tray by spraying it with a little oil.

Place as many kebabs in the air fryer as will comfortably fit, then air fry for 10 minutes, turning them 2–3 times, until slightly blackened at the edges.

Meanwhile, add all the ingredients for the dipping sauce to a small saucepan, mix well and place over a medium heat. Bring to the boil and simmer for 10 minutes until thickened.

**continued overleaf**

**continued overleaf**

**For the dipping sauce**

- 75g (⅓ cup) crunchy peanut butter
- ½ tsp lemongrass paste
- ½ tsp ground coriander
- ½ tsp dried chilli flakes
- 100ml (generous ⅓ cup) water
- 1 tbsp garlic-infused oil
- 1 tsp palm sugar or light brown sugar
- 1 tsp tamarind paste
- ¼ tsp salt

Remove the skewers from the air fryer and allow to rest for 5 minutes, then repeat for any skewers that wouldn't fit into the air fryer.

Serve the skewers with the cucumber ribbons and dipping sauce and some steamed or coconut rice.

## TIPS

Chicken breast mini fillets would also work perfectly instead of chicken thighs, if you prefer – just shave a couple of minutes off the cooking time.

As I touched on in the recipe intro, all of the ingredients used here can be easily found in supermarkets. You'll find spices such as turmeric, ground coriander, paprika and chilli flakes with all the other spices, no problem. Lemongrass paste, galangal/ginger paste, tamarind paste and palm sugar are also very likely to be nearby in the spice aisle and usually come in either small plastic tubes or tiny jars (check the Asian cooking ingredients shelves too if you can't find them). When it comes to ginger paste, be sure to check the international aisle as you can often find a huge jar of it, which is much better value than buying a small jar!

# SPICY BEAN BURGERS

 Serve with vegan-friendly mayo.

 Once cooked and cooled, freeze for up to 3 months. Air fry from frozen at 180°C/350°F for 7-8 minutes until piping hot.

- ½ x 400g (14oz) can of kidney beans, drained
- ½ x 400g (14oz) can of haricot (navy) beans, drained, reserving 100ml (generous ⅓ cup) of the water from the can
- 200g (7oz) frozen mixed veg (such as sweetcorn, peas, green beans and carrots)
- 1 tbsp water
- 1 tbsp garlic-infused oil
- 1 tsp tomato purée (paste)
- 1 tsp smoked paprika
- 1 tsp ground cumin
- ½ tsp cayenne pepper
- 1 tsp dried mixed herbs
- ½ tsp salt
- 4 tbsp gluten-free plain (all-purpose) flour
- 75g (1¼ cups) gluten-free breadcrumbs, plus an extra 120g (2 cups) to coat
- Vegetable oil in a spray bottle, for greasing

## To serve
- 5 gluten-free burger buns
- 2 handfuls of iceberg lettuce, shredded
- 5 tsp mayonnaise
- 1 extra-large avocado, mashed with a pinch each of salt and ground black pepper

**Makes 5 / Takes 25 minutes**

**You know when you occasionally think of friends that you've lost touch with over the years and then wonder how on Earth things ended up this way? Well that's exactly how I feel about spicy bean burgers in a crispy coating of golden breadcrumbs – perhaps even to a stronger degree. As they always contain either gluten, onion and/or garlic, it's been something ridiculous like 15 years since I last ate one. Let's just say that, after making my own, the reunion was so emotional that I might just be inspired enough to message my old school friends and see how they're doing. (Pictured overleaf.)**

Place the drained kidney and haricot beans in a large bowl (don't forget to reserve some of the liquid from the haricot can!). Mash with a potato masher until all of the kidney beans are broken and many of the haricot beans are roughly broken.

Place the frozen mixed veg into a suitably sized, microwave-safe bowl and add the water. Loosely cover with a plate and microwave for 5 minutes on full power (900W) until completely cooked through. Drain and transfer to a chopping board, then use a sharp knife to chop up any larger pieces, ensuring they're all roughly the same size as the peas and sweetcorn. Transfer to the bowl of crushed beans.

Add the remaining ingredients to the bowl, along with the reserved bean water. Mix for around a minute until everything is combined and evenly dispersed. Set aside to rest for 5–10 minutes to allow the breadcrumbs and flour to hydrate and the mixture to become a little more sticky. Meanwhile, spread the extra breadcrumbs out on a large dinner plate.

Take a tennis-ball-sized portion of the mixture (around a fifth of the total mixture) and roll into a tight ball. Flatten between your hands to form a patty around 2cm (¾ inch) thick. Compress any loose pieces back into the patty, then place on the plate of breadcrumbs.

Without disturbing the patty too much and keeping it mostly in place, spoon breadcrumbs over the top and up the sides and then gently press them to the patty so that they stick.

Heat or preheat the air fryer to 180°C/350°F. Generously grease the base of the air fryer basket or crisping tray by spraying it with oil.

Transfer the burger to the air fryer and repeat for as many burgers that will comfortably fit into the air fryer without touching. Spray generously with oil and air fry for 12 minutes, flipping them over halfway through and generously spraying once more with oil, until the breadcrumbs are golden. Repeat with the rest of the burgers.

Serve in the burger buns with shredded iceberg, mayo and smashed avocado, alongside some sweet potato fries (page 41) and onion rings (page 181).

## TIP

The use of store-bought gluten-free breadcrumbs is especially important in the bean burgers for binding purposes – using blitzed fresh gluten-free bread isn't recommended as it's far too absorbent and will turn to mush when hydrated! See page 24 for further explanation on my recommendation of store-bought gluten-free breadcrumbs.

# 30-MINUTE PEPPERONI CALZONE

 Use lactose-free Greek yoghurt.

 Use a thick dairy-free yoghurt and a dairy-free cheese that melts well.

 Use FODMAP-friendly pepperoni and lactose-free Greek yoghurt.

Use courgette (zucchini), sliced into rounds 5mm (¼ inch) thick, drizzled with olive oil and air fried for 12 minutes, turning halfway through, instead of pepperoni.

 Combine the dairy-free and veggie advice, and brush with sweetened almond milk instead of egg.

 Once cooked and cooled, freeze for up to 3 months. Air fry from frozen at 180°C/350°F for 10–12 minutes until piping hot in the middle.

- 150ml (⅝ cup) tomato passata
- 1½ tsp dried oregano
- 1 tsp garlic-infused oil, plus extra to drizzle
- ¼ tsp each of salt and ground black pepper
- 250g (1¾ cups) gluten-free self-raising flour, plus extra for dusting
- 260g (1¼ cups) Greek yoghurt
- 125g (4½oz) mozzarella, thinly sliced
- Handful of basil leaves, roughly chopped
- 9 slices of pepperoni
- 1 small egg, beaten

**Makes 3 / Takes 30 minutes**

**As you'll soon discover, your air fryer has a secret side hustle: moonlighting as a mini pizza oven! So why not give it a test run by making my pepperoni calzone? It's essentially a pepperoni pizza pasty that's packed with a rich tomato sauce, gooey mozzarella and pepperoni. Perhaps best of all, there's no yeast or proving required so it can be on the table in less than 30 minutes.**

To make the pizza sauce, grab a small bowl and mix together the passata, oregano, garlic-infused oil, salt and pepper. Set aside.

Add the flour and Greek yoghurt (give it a good stir before using) to a large bowl. Mix thoroughly using a spatula to ensure there are no hidden clumps of yoghurt-coated flour. As it starts to come together, use your hands to bring it together into a slightly sticky ball.

Knead the dough briefly in the bowl until smooth, combined and no longer sticky. Dough still too sticky? Add a little more flour. Dough too dry? Add a little water.

Transfer the dough to a medium sheet of lightly floured non-stick baking parchment. Divide the dough into 3 equal portions and roll each into a ball. Place 2 back in the bowl, and cover.

Lightly flour the rolling pin and roll out the remaining ball into a circle, aiming for a 3mm (⅛ inch) thickness, ensuring it's symmetrical and an even thickness all over. Re-flour the rolling pin as necessary to stop it from sticking to the dough.

In the bottom third of the rolled out dough, leaving a 2cm (¾ inch) gap between the filling and the edge of the dough, add a third of the sliced mozzarella, followed by a third of the basil, 3 slices of pepperoni, a quarter of the pizza sauce and a drizzle of garlic-infused oil.

Brush the edges of the dough lightly with a little water to help them stick together. Fold over the empty side of the dough so that it's 5mm (¼ inch) short of meeting the edge of the filled side. It should form a neat semi-circle shape. Remember that this dough has no tolerance for stretching so be sure to simply fold it over – don't pull and stretch it over as you fold!

**continued overleaf**

Crimp the edge of the calzone shut by folding and pinching multiple times all along the seam. Brush all over with some of the beaten egg.

Use a sharp knife to cut 3 slits in the calzone and trim the paper around the calzone, ensuring you leave no more than 1cm (½ inch) of excess paper. Repeat with the rest of the dough portions and filling (reserving the last quarter of pizza sauce for later), so you have 3 prepared calzone, each on its own sheet of baking parchment.

Heat or preheat the air fryer to 180°C/350°F.

Lift one calzone into the air fryer (or as many as will comfortably fit at once), using the baking parchment to ferry it in, and air fry for 12–14 minutes until golden. Use the back of a spoon to add a thin smearing of the remaining pizza sauce all over the top of the calzone 4 minutes before it's done. Repeat for the remaining calzone and serve alongside some rocket (arugula).

# TURKEY DINOSAURS

 Serve with FODMAP-friendly sides.

 Once cooked and cooled, freeze for up to 3 months. Air fry from frozen at 200°C/400°F for 7-8 minutes. Check internal temp with a digital food thermometer against those given on page 30.

- 500g (1lb 2oz) minced (ground) turkey breast
- 1 tsp salt
- ½ tsp ground white or black pepper
- 60g (scant ½ cup) gluten-free plain (all-purpose) flour, plus 70g (generous ½ cup) for the final coating
- 2 large eggs
- 40g (⅜ cup) gluten-free breadcrumbs
- Pinch of ground turmeric
- Vegetable oil in a spray bottle, for greasing

**To serve**
- Homemade or store-bought mashed potato, warmed
- 1 x 400g (14oz) can of baked (Boston) beans, warmed
- 250g (2 cups) frozen peas, cooked

**Serves 3–4 (makes 9–10) / Takes 25 minutes + freezing**

**I heard that it would be impossible to bring dinosaurs back to life, so the least I can do is bring back turkey dinosaurs for gluten-free folks. After all, it feels like 65 million years ago since I last ate one... Now, some might say that making these seems like quite an extreme length to go to just for a turkey dinosaur, but I know deep in my heart that there are a lot of people out there who would quite happily do a lot more just to see them back on our plates!**

Add the turkey, salt and pepper to a large bowl, and mix with a wooden spoon until everything is super-smooth and there's no more texture visible in the mince.

Loosely line a baking tray (30 x 25cm/12 x 10 inches) with a large sheet of non-stick baking parchment. Place the turkey on top of it and pat into a flat layer, using a silicone spatula or the back of a wooden spoon. Place another large sheet of baking parchment on top and continue to flatten the turkey, using your hands, until it's about 1.5cm (⅔ inch) thick. Check by peeking under the baking parchment that it's not thinner or thicker in places.

Place in the freezer for 1½–2 hours to firm up; we want it partially frozen for the next step, not frozen solid!

Remove from the freezer and peel off the top layer of baking parchment. Use 12cm (5 inch) dinosaur biscuit cutters to cut out as many dinosaur shapes as you can, as close together as possible. Gently apply pressure and very, very slightly twist to ensure they're separated. Leave them in place on the tray, and remove the excess turkey between the shapes; set this aside.

Place the shapes back in the freezer on the tray for 30–60 minutes; this time, they should be near frozen solid when they come out.

Meanwhile, use up the excess turkey mince. Line another similar-sized baking tray with a large sheet of baking parchment.

**continued overleaf**

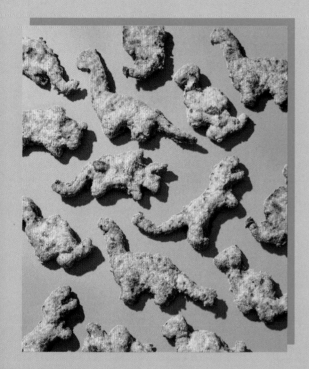

Place all the offcuts in a small pile and cover with another sheet of baking parchment, then allow to defrost a little until the mince can be squashed and patted back down into a 1.5cm (⅔ inch) thick layer – it can take anywhere from 15 to 30 minutes before it is defrosted enough, but there's no need to let it completely thaw. Once patted down into an even layer again, cut out more dinosaur shapes and discard the excess, then place the extra shapes in the freezer too.

Once the shapes are frozen enough that you can pick them up without bending or flexing, they're ready to coat. Spread the 60g (scant ½ cup) of flour out on a dinner plate, beat the eggs in a small, wide bowl, then spread the 70g (generous ½ cup) of flour, the breadcrumbs and turmeric out on another dinner plate and gently mix together.

Remove the first tray of dinosaur shapes from the freezer, then roll each in the plain flour until well coated, dip in the beaten egg mixture, then dredge in the flour and breadcrumb mixture until completely coated.

Heat or preheat the air fryer to 200°C/400°F. Generously grease the base of the air fryer basket or crisping tray by spraying it with oil. Add as many turkey dinosaurs to the air fryer as will comfortably fit without touching, and air fry for 12 minutes, flipping them halfway through and spraying generously with oil once more, or until golden with a crisp coating, especially in the middle. Repeat, using any remaining coated shapes, then repeat the coating and air frying process for the rest of the shapes on the second tray in the freezer.

Celebrate the return of turkey dinosaurs into your life by making a volcano out of mashed potato with baked-bean lava, and peas on the side.

# 20-MINUTE KOFTA KEBABS

 Use a thick dairy-free yoghurt.

 Use lactose-free Greek yoghurt.

 See lactose-free advice.

 Once cooked and cooled, freeze for up to 3 months. Air fry from frozen at 180°C/350°F for 7-8 minutes. Check internal temp with a digital food thermometer against those given on page 30.

## For the koftas

- 250g (9oz) minced (ground) lamb
- 250g (9oz) minced (ground) beef
- 2 tbsp gluten-free plain (all-purpose) flour
- 1 tsp ground cumin
- 1 tsp smoked paprika
- 1 tsp ground allspice
- 1 tsp cayenne pepper
- 1 tsp salt
- ½ tsp ground cinnamon
- Small handful of parsley, roughly chopped
- Vegetable oil in a spray bottle, for greasing

## For the yoghurt sauce

- 100g (scant 1 cup) Greek yoghurt
- 1 tbsp garlic-infused oil
- ½ tsp ground cinnamon
- 2 tbsp lemon juice
- Pinch each of salt and ground black pepper
- 2 tsp finely chopped chives

**Serves 3 (makes 6 kebabs) / Takes 20 minutes**

**This recipe is testament to the air fryer's uncanny ability to achieve a BBQ-like finish on my beef and lamb kofta kebabs. When paired with the thick and creamy yoghurt sauce and gluten-free flatbreads (store-bought, or see page 186 for homemade), this is a super-speedy crowd-pleaser that you'll never make in the oven again.**

In a large bowl, combine all the ingredients for the koftas and mix well, until the minced meat is smooth and everything is evenly dispersed.

Separate the mixture into 12 equal balls (mine were 45g/1½oz each) and form each into a little sausage shape. Grab 6 wooden or metal skewers – most importantly, they need to fit into your air fryer, so check that they do first. Wooden skewers can be trimmed to fit. Thread 2 koftas onto each skewer.

Heat or preheat the air fryer to 200°C/400°F. Lightly grease the base of the air fryer basket or crisping tray by spraying it with a little oil.

Place as many kebabs in the air fryer as will comfortably fit, then air fry for 7–8 minutes, turning them halfway through, until golden and seared. Meanwhile, in a small dish, mix together the ingredients for the sauce until smooth.

Remove the koftas from the air fryer and allow to rest for 5 minutes, then repeat for any that wouldn't fit.

Serve with the yoghurt sauce, a herby salad and some chilli sauce, if you like, and store-bought gluten-free flatbreads or my mozzarella-stuffed flatbreads (page 186).

## TIP

If you're feeling lazy or lack skewers, simply air fry the meat mixture once divided into 12 balls at 180°C/350°F for 15 minutes, turning them halfway through.

# 5-INGREDIENT STICKY HONEY MUSTARD GAMMON

 Use maple syrup instead of honey.

 Once cooked and cooled, slice and freeze for up to 3 months. Air fry slices from frozen at 180°C/350°F for 5-6 minutes. Check internal temp with a digital food thermometer against those given on page 30.

- 750g-1kg (1lb 10oz-2lb 3oz) unsmoked boneless gammon joint
- 1 litre (generous 4 cups) pineapple juice
- 4 tbsp honey
- 1 tbsp Dijon mustard
- ½ tsp ground cinnamon

**Serves 4-6 / Takes 60 minutes + resting**

**Transforming a humble gammon joint into a triumphantly sticky, sweet, cinnamon-tinged ham couldn't be simpler. Simply simmer, air fry, slice and pair with crispy roast potatoes (page 44) alongside your favourite veggies (page 175), for the ultimate lazy centrepiece to remember.**

Place the gammon in a medium saucepan and pour in the pineapple juice – if it doesn't cover the gammon, then either use a smaller saucepan or top it up with water. Bring to the boil and then allow to lightly simmer for around 30–40 minutes.

Remove from the pan and transfer to a medium sheet of foil, orientating the gammon so it's 'standing up'.

If your gammon has a layer of skin on top, remove the skin and most of the fat beneath using a sharp knife, leaving a thin fat layer. Score the remaining fat in a criss-cross fashion. Smaller gammon joints have often already had the skin removed, so skip this part if your gammon looks pretty 'naked' already.

In a small bowl, mix together the honey, mustard, cinnamon and 2 tablespoons of the pineapple juice from the saucepan. Brush it all over the top and the sides of the gammon, then loosely close the foil around it.

Heat or preheat the air fryer to 170°C/340°F. Air fry the gammon for 15 minutes, then open the foil and brush with more of the glaze. Air fry for a further 5 minutes until golden, sticky and slightly blackened at the edges.

Allow to rest for 10 minutes, then slice and serve alongside roast potatoes (page 44), carrot and swede mash, or air fried veggies of your choice (page 175).

# CHEAT'S CHEESY CHICKEN KYIV

 Use dairy-free cream cheese and a smoked dairy-free cheese.

 Use lactose-free cream cheese.

 See low lactose advice.

 Once cooked and cooled, freeze for up to 3 months. Air fry from frozen at 180°C/350°F for 7-8 minutes. Check internal temp with a digital food thermometer against those given on page 30.

- 3 tbsp cream cheese
- 1 tbsp garlic-infused oil
- 1 tsp finely chopped parsley
- 1 tbsp finely grated Red Leicester cheese
- 4 tbsp gluten-free plain (all-purpose) flour or cornflour (cornstarch)
- 1 large egg
- 70g (generous 1 cup) gluten-free breadcrumbs
- 2 medium skinless chicken breast fillets (250g/9oz in total)
- Vegetable oil in a spray bottle, for greasing

**Serves 2 / Takes 20 minutes**

Though this is a 'cheat's' version of a chicken Kyiv, you'd really be hard pressed to notice much of a difference. In reality, the only cheat here is that we're technically stuffing the chicken breasts instead of pounding them, butterflying them, filling them and rolling them up, then somehow sealing them up again. I'm sure you can see why I use the stuffing method instead! With a creamy, cheesy filling and a hint of garlic, this recipe will nullify the fact that a decent gluten-free chicken Kyiv is hard to come by.

Combine the cream cheese, garlic-infused oil, parsley and grated cheese in a small dish. Spread the flour over a plate, beat the egg in a small bowl, then spread the breadcrumbs out on a second plate.

Lay the chicken breasts flat on a chopping board. Holding a sharp knife at around 45 degrees, create a deep slit in each breast, leaving at least 1cm (½ inch) above and below the slit – make sure you don't cut all the way through! Fill the slits in the chicken breasts with the filling. Use the back of a spoon or your fingers to push the filling into the slit so that as little of the filling as possible is visible.

Roll one filled chicken breast in the flour until lightly dusted on both sides. Next, coat well in beaten egg, then roll in the breadcrumbs until tightly coated. Repeat with the other breast.

Heat or preheat the air fryer to 180°C/350°F. Generously grease the base of the air fryer basket or crisping tray by spraying it with oil. Add the coated chicken breasts to the air fryer and generously spray the tops with oil. Air fry for 15 minutes, turning them halfway through and spraying generously once more with oil, until the breadcrumbs are golden brown.

Serve alongside air fryer chips, fries or wedges (page 38), air fried veggies of your choice (page 175), smashed or hasselback potatoes (page 47) and salad.

## TIP

To make crispy potato cubes like in the photo, simply chop potatoes into 2cm (¾ inch) cubes, spray with oil and air fry at 200°C/400°F for 15-20 minutes, turning halfway.

# STICKY HONEY MUSTARD SAUSAGE 'TRAYBAKE'

 Use maple syrup instead of honey and use FODMAP-friendly sausages.

 Use gluten-free vegetarian sausages.

 Use gluten-free vegan-friendly sausages and maple syrup instead of honey.

 Once cooked and cooled, freeze for up to 3 months. Air fry from frozen at 180°C/350°F for 9-10 minutes. Check internal temp of the sausages with a digital food thermometer against those given on page 30.

- 2 medium potatoes (450g/1lb in total), unpeeled, chopped into 1cm (½ inch) cubes
- 2 medium carrots (250g/9oz in total), chopped into 1cm (½ inch) cubes
- 1 red (bell) pepper, deseeded and chopped into 5cm (2 inch) chunks
- 3 tbsp garlic-infused oil
- ½ tsp each of salt and ground black pepper
- 6 gluten-free pork sausages
- 2 tbsp honey
- 2 tsp wholegrain mustard
- Small handful of finely chopped chives

**Serves 3 / Takes 30 minutes**

**This sticky sausage, roasted carrot, red pepper and potato traybake is so miraculous that you won't even need a baking tray to make it! It's the ultimate all-in-one lazy dinner that only really requires you to chop up some veg and turn everything over occasionally to ensure it's all cooking evenly.**

Add the potatoes, carrots and red pepper to a large bowl, followed by the garlic-infused oil, salt and pepper. Stir well until everything is coated.

Heat or preheat the air fryer to 180°C/350°F. Add the veggies, spread them out into an even layer and air fry for 15 minutes, turning them over halfway through.

Turn all of the veg over once more, then add the sausages on top and air fry for 10–12 minutes, turning everything over halfway through, or until the sausages are nicely browned on both sides.

Meanwhile, mix the honey and mustard in a small dish.

Drizzle the honey-mustard over the top of everything and turn it all over until well coated. Air fry for a further 2–3 minutes, then sprinkle with chives and serve.

# CHEAT'S FALAFEL AND TAHINI SAUCE

Serves 3-4 (makes 14) / Takes 20 minutes

 **V**

 **DF** Use a thick dairy-free yoghurt.

 **LF** Use lactose-free Greek yoghurt.

 **VE** See dairy-free advice.

 ❄ Once cooked and cooled, freeze for up to 3 months. Air fry from frozen at 180°C/350°F for 8-9 minutes.

- Vegetable oil in a spray bottle, for greasing
- Salt and ground black pepper

**For the falafel**
- 400g (14oz) can of chickpeas, drained, reserving 60ml (¼ cup) of the liquid from the can
- 50g (1¾oz) spring onion (scallion) greens, roughly chopped
- ½ tsp cayenne pepper
- 2 tsp ground cumin
- 1 tsp ground coriander
- ½ tsp bicarbonate of soda (baking soda)
- 1 tsp lemon juice
- 1 tbsp garlic-infused oil
- Handful of chopped parsley
- Handful of chopped coriander (cilantro)
- 100g (generous 1½ cups) gluten-free breadcrumbs (page 24)
- 2 tbsp gluten-free plain (all-purpose) flour

**For the tahini sauce**
- 140g (⅔ cup) Greek yoghurt
- 1 tbsp tahini
- 1 tbsp garlic-infused oil
- 2 tsp lemon juice

**Whenever I fancy falafel, it's always served with a flatbread I can't eat, and when I'm in supermarkets, the most readily available falafel always contains wheat! Fortunately, my food processor makes making my own an absolute breeze and the air fryer never fails to deliver the perfect, crispy finish. As I'm never organized enough to make falafel 'properly', using dried chickpeas and soaking them overnight, I often rely on my 'cheat's' version which uses canned chickpeas instead. So if that sounds like you, too, then this recipe has you covered!**

Add all the ingredients for the falafel (including the reserved water from the chickpea can and ½ teaspoon of salt) to a food processor. Pulse for around 20 seconds or until everything has been broken down and a smooth 'dough' with visible breadcrumbs forms.

Heat or preheat the air fryer to 180°C/350°F. Generously grease the base of the air fryer basket or crisping tray by spraying it with oil.

Use an ice-cream scoop to portion out the falafel mixture and roll into balls (about 40g/1½oz each). Place as many as will comfortably fit into the air fryer without touching, and spray generously with oil. Flatten them down with the back of a spoon until they're around 1.5cm (⅔ inch) thick and air fry for 10 minutes, flipping them over halfway through and spraying once more with oil, until golden on the outside. Repeat with any leftover falafel mixture.

Meanwhile, in a small dish, mix together the ingredients for the sauce until smooth, then season with salt and black pepper.

I like to serve this in bowls with shredded lettuce and the tahini sauce drizzled over. Sprinkle over some dried chilli flakes too, if you like. Serve with tortilla wraps, or my gluten-free mozzarella-stuffed flatbreads (page 186) for scooping.

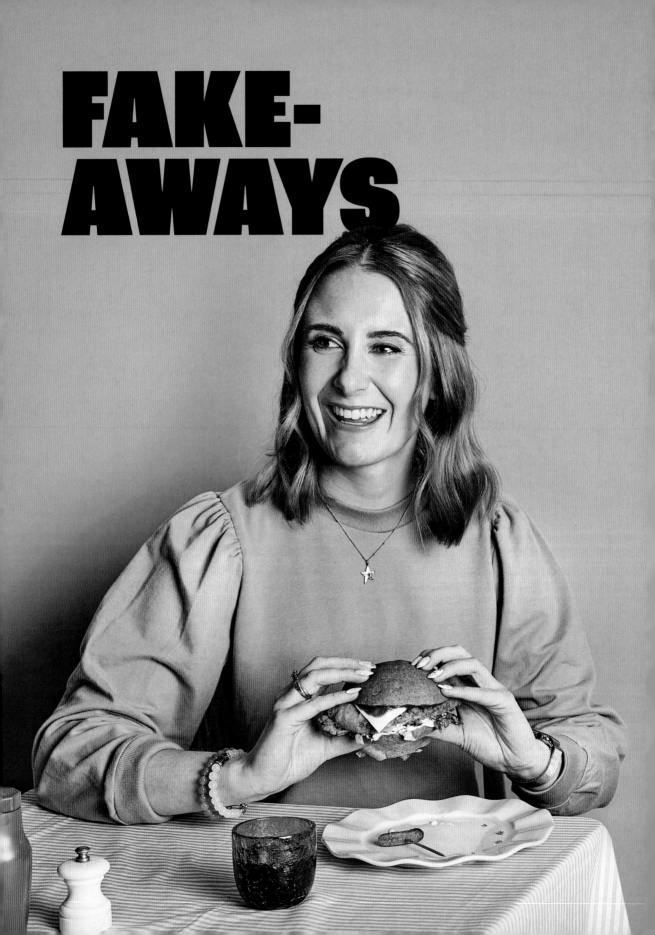

# FAKE-AWAYS

When ordering from a takeaway it sometimes feels more stressful than helpful or convenient (sadly, a common feeling when you're gluten-free). If you feel the same, look no further than your own air fryer. OK, you might have to look a little further – namely to the stove – for a helping hand, but in most cases, the air fryer has got you covered from start to finish.

Best of all, the air fryer is the fastest way to that golden, fried fakeaway finish, with a few modest spritzes of oil going a very long way. Think flaky air fried fish or golden chicken nuggets, crispy shredded duck chow mein and chicken shawarma kebabs that taste like they've been flame-grilled, as well as pizza that has that 'fresh out of the pizza oven' flavour.

Not only can recreating all of your takeaway favourites in an air fryer save you money, but it's undoubtedly where you can make them healthier too. It wasn't until I started writing this chapter that I realized how many of the takeaways dishes I missed were deep-fried! Fortunately, your air fryer means there's no need for deep-frying at all, so you can now enjoy all your most-loved dishes more often.

# FISH AND CHIPS

Ensure all serving accompaniments are FODMAP-friendly.

❄ Once cooked and cooled, freeze for up to 3 months. Air fry from frozen at 180°C/350°F for 6-7 minutes. Check internal temp with a digital food thermometer against those given on page 30.

- 1 quantity of air fryer chips (fries), prepared as described on page 38, omitting the spice blend
- Vegetable oil in a spray bottle, for greasing
- 4 tbsp gluten-free plain (all-purpose) flour or cornflour (cornstarch)
- 1 tsp salt
- ½ tsp ground black or white pepper
- 1 large egg
- 65g (2¼oz) gluten-free cornflakes
- 2 skinless, boneless cod or basa fillets

**To serve**
- Tomato ketchup, tartare sauce and vinegar (ensure gluten-free)
- 1 x 400g (14oz) can of mushy peas, heated

**Serves 2 / Takes 20-30 minutes**

**I've tried all manner of different crispy coatings on my air fried fish over the years and without a doubt a cornflake coating takes the prize for the best finish! Plus, as cornflakes are already super crunchy, you don't necessarily need to use much oil to achieve that finish. Cod is a classic choice, but with prices shooting through the roof, basa is a great alternative that'll save a few precious pennies.**

Heat or preheat the air fryer to 200°C/400°F.

Place the prepared chips in the air fryer and follow the timings on page 40. If your air fryer has one drawer/compartment for cooking, once finished, remove the chips (keep warm until later or briefly reheat once the fish is done) while you air fry the fish. If your air fryer has two drawers, then generously grease the base of the second drawer's air fryer basket or crisping tray by spraying it with oil, ready for the fish.

Mix the flour, salt and pepper on a large dinner plate. Briefly beat the egg with a fork in a medium bowl. Place the cornflakes into a large bowl and use the end of a rolling pin to bash them until consistently fine. Ensure there are no whole cornflakes left or they won't stick to the fish very well.

Dredge the fish fillets in the flour until evenly dusted on both sides, then dip into the egg until well coated. Finally, dredge them in the cornflakes, ensuring even coverage on both sides, gently squeezing and compacting the cornflakes to the fillets.

If you have a single-drawer air fryer, once the chips are done and removed, add the coated fish to the air fryer. If you have a two-drawer air fryer, add the coated fish to the second drawer. Spray all over with oil and air fry for 8-10 minutes (no need to flip) until beginning to turn golden brown in places.

Serve with ketchup, tartare sauce, vinegar and mushy peas.

# MARK'S SWEET AND SOUR PORK OR CHICKEN

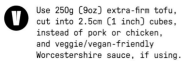 Use 250g (9oz) extra-firm tofu, cut into 2.5cm (1 inch) cubes, instead of pork or chicken, and veggie/vegan-friendly Worcestershire sauce, if using.

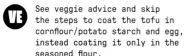 See veggie advice and skip the steps to coat the tofu in cornflour/potato starch and egg, instead coating it only in the seasoned flour.

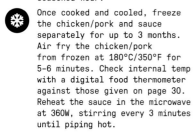 Once cooked and cooled, freeze the chicken/pork and sauce separately for up to 3 months. Air fry the chicken/pork from frozen at 180°C/350°F for 5-6 minutes. Check internal temp with a digital food thermometer against those given on page 30. Reheat the sauce in the microwave at 360W, stirring every 3 minutes until piping hot.

- 300g (10½oz) skinless chicken breast fillet or pork tenderloin fillet, chopped into 2.5cm (1 inch) chunks
- Vegetable oil in a spray bottle, for greasing
- 2 tbsp garlic-infused oil
- 1 large red (bell) pepper, deseeded and chopped into 2cm (¾ inch) squares
- 150g (5½oz) fresh or canned pineapple, in chunks
- 1 tbsp cornflour (cornstarch) or potato starch
- Handful of spring onion (scallion) greens, chopped

**continued overleaf**

---

**Serves 3-4 / Takes 25 minutes**

**This is an 'air fryer-ified' version of Mark's Cantonese-style sweet and sour from my book *How to Plan Anything Gluten Free*. The pork/chicken isn't deep-fried so is much healthier yet just as crisp, but don't be fooled into thinking you can use next to no oil for this recipe. That crisp coating needs it to form a batter; otherwise, you'll be left with lots of white, floury looking pork or chicken!**

For the batter, beat the eggs with a fork in a medium bowl, then set aside. Spread out the cornflour or potato starch on a large dinner plate. Add the flour, baking powder, pepper and salt to a large bowl and give it a good mix.

Place half the chicken or pork pieces on the cornflour/potato starch plate and gently toss around until well coated. Transfer the coated pieces to the beaten egg bowl and turn them until completely covered. Next, transfer the pieces to the seasoned flour bowl and roll around until completely coated. Repeat with the other half of the chicken or pork.

Heat or preheat the air fryer to 200°C/400°F. Generously grease the base of the air fryer basket or crisping tray by spraying it with vegetable oil.

Place the coated chicken/pork pieces in the air fryer basket, ensuring they are not touching, and generously spray with oil. Remember, any white floury patches will stay that way unless you spray them with oil. Air fry for 8–10 minutes, flipping them halfway through and spraying any white patches once more with oil. Keep warm in the air fryer, with the door half open, until later.

For the sauce, add all the ingredients to a small bowl and give them a good mix until well combined.

Place a large wok over a medium heat on the stove and add the garlic-infused oil. Once heated, add the red pepper and stir fry for 3 minutes.

**continued overleaf**

**For the batter**

- 2 medium eggs
- 40g (⅓ cup) cornflour (cornstarch) or potato starch
- 100g (¾ cup) gluten-free plain (all-purpose) flour
- ½ tsp gluten-free baking powder
- ½ tsp ground white or black pepper
- 1 tsp salt

**For the sweet and sour sauce**

- 100g (3½oz) tomato ketchup
- 1 tbsp gluten-free soy sauce
- 80g (½ cup minus 2 tbsp) light brown or caster (superfine) sugar
- 1 tbsp ginger paste
- 2 tbsp white rice vinegar
- 230ml (1 cup minus 2 tsp) water
- 2 tbsp gluten-free Worcestershire sauce (optional)

Add the pineapple chunks and stir fry for 1 more minute. Next, add the tablespoon of cornflour or potato starch and mix immediately so that everything is nicely coated.

Once coated, add the sweet and sour sauce. Give it a good stir until all the lumps of flour are gone. Bring to the boil, then allow the sauce to simmer for 2–3 minutes until it begins to thicken.

Throw in the coated chicken or pork pieces and stir in until well coated in the sauce. Top with the spring onion greens and serve immediately with egg-fried rice (page 165).

**TIP**

The crispy coating on the pork or chicken can begin to soften a little if left to keep warm in the air fryer for too long. If this is the case, simply air fry for 1–2 minutes to reheat and regain that crisp coating before adding to the sauce.

# CHICKEN KATSU CURRY

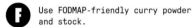 Use FODMAP-friendly curry powder and stock.

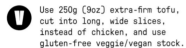 Use 250g (9oz) extra-firm tofu, cut into long, wide slices, instead of chicken, and use gluten-free veggie/vegan stock.

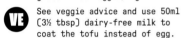 See veggie advice and use 50ml (3½ tbsp) dairy-free milk to coat the tofu instead of egg.

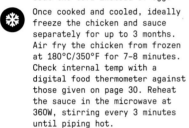 Once cooked and cooled, ideally freeze the chicken and sauce separately for up to 3 months. Air fry the chicken from frozen at 180°C/350°F for 7-8 minutes. Check internal temp with a digital food thermometer against those given on page 30. Reheat the sauce in the microwave at 360W, stirring every 3 minutes until piping hot.

## For the katsu sauce

- 2 tbsp garlic-infused oil
- 2 carrots, thinly sliced
- 1½ tbsp gluten-free plain (all-purpose) flour or cornflour (cornstarch)
- 3 tsp mild curry powder
- 600ml (2½ cups) gluten-free chicken stock
- 4 tsp gluten-free soy sauce
- 2 dried bay leaves
- 1 tsp garam masala
- Handful of chives, finely chopped, to serve (optional)

**continued overleaf**

---

**Serves 2 / Takes 25 minutes**

**Here's yet another fakeaway classic that featured in my first book, *How to Make Anything Gluten Free*, but is tweaked here especially for the air fryer. Crushed cornflakes more closely recreate the panko breadcrumb coating you'd usually find on katsu chicken and, as you might know already, a cornflake crumb comes out especially well in the air fryer without the need for loads of oil.**

For the katsu sauce, heat the garlic-infused oil in a large pan over a medium heat. Add the carrots and fry for 2–3 minutes until slightly softened. Add the flour and curry powder. Mix well until all the carrots are coated and continue to cook for 1 minute.

Add the stock, soy sauce and bay leaves, bring to the boil, then turn down the heat and simmer for 20 minutes or until the sauce thickens. Once the sauce is nice and thick, yet still a pourable consistency, stir in the garam masala. Remove from the heat and discard the bay leaves. Traditionally, you'd then strain the sauce to remove the carrots, but you can leave them in if you like – they taste great!

While the sauce is simmering and thickening, prepare the chicken. Butterfly each breast fillet carefully, using a sharp knife: lay them flat and slice horizontally so you can open each like a book, being careful not to cut all the way through! If you're not familiar with this technique (you could search online), you can always place the chicken breasts between 2 sheets of cling film (plastic wrap) and bash until flat with a rolling pin or meat mallet. Either way, we're aiming to make the chicken as flat as possible so it'll get more of that crispy coating and cook twice as fast.

Spread the cornflour, salt and pepper out onto a large dinner plate, ensuring it is nicely mixed. Briefly beat the egg in a medium bowl with a fork. Place the cornflakes into a large bowl and use the end of a rolling pin to bash them until consistently fine. Ensure there are no whole cornflakes left or they won't stick to the chicken very well!

**continued overleaf**

**For the chicken**

- 2 skinless chicken breast fillets
- 5 tbsp cornflour (cornstarch)
- 1 tsp salt
- ½ tsp ground black or white pepper
- 1 large egg
- 80g (2¾oz) gluten-free cornflakes
- Vegetable oil in a spray bottle, for greasing
- ¼ tsp dried chilli flakes, to serve (optional)

Dredge the prepared chicken on the flour plate until evenly dusted on both sides, then dip into the egg bowl until well coated. Finally, dredge in the cornflake bowl, ensuring even, tight coverage on both sides, gently squeezing and compacting the cornflakes onto the chicken.

Heat or preheat the air fryer to 200°C/400°F. Lightly grease the base of the air fryer basket or crisping tray by spraying it with a little oil.

Place the prepared chicken in the air fryer basket and spray with oil, making sure they are touching as little as possible (or air fry in separate air fryer drawers if space is lacking). Air fry for 11–12 minutes until the cornflake crumb is crisp and golden brown in places, turning them over halfway through and spraying with oil once more. Allow to cool for 5–10 minutes before slicing, then use a sharp knife to cut each into 1cm (½ inch) strips.

Serve the crispy chicken on top of sticky jasmine rice alongside the sauce, then sprinkle with chives and dried chilli flakes, if using. If you opted not to strain the sauce, don't forget to remove the bay leaves before serving.

# SALT AND PEPPER CHICKEN SPICE BAG

Use 250g (9oz) extra-firm tofu, cut into 2.5cm (1 inch) cubes instead of chicken.

See veggie advice.

Once cooked and cooled, freeze for up to 3 months. Air fry from frozen at 180°C/350°F for 6-7 minutes. Check internal temp of the chicken with a digital food thermometer against those given on page 30.

- 600g (1lb 5oz) Maris Piper potatoes, skin on or off, cut into strips 1cm (½ inch) wide and 4mm (⅛ inch) thick
- 3 tbsp vegetable or olive oil, plus extra in a spray bottle for greasing
- 2 tbsp gluten-free plain (all-purpose) flour or cornflour (cornstarch), plus 6 tbsp to coat the chicken
- 1 red (bell) pepper, deseeded and chopped into 2.5cm (1 inch) chunks
- 300g (10½oz) chicken breast mini fillets, chopped into long, very thin strips
- 1 tbsp garlic-infused oil
- Small handful of spring onion (scallion) greens, finely chopped

### For the spice mix
- ¾ tsp Chinese five spice powder
- ¾ tsp ground ginger
- ½ tsp dried chilli flakes
- 1 tsp salt
- ¼ tsp ground black pepper

**Meet an Irish take on Chinese takeaway that fuses two legendary favourites (salt and pepper chicken and salt and pepper chips) to create an all-in-one plate of pure awesomeness. After all, when such an ingenious creation exists, why should we let gluten get in the way like it always does? So here's my own version, which I genuinely can't believe isn't deep-fried!**

Heat or preheat the air fryer to 200°C/400°F

Add the potato strips to a medium bowl, followed by the oil. Mix well, then add the 2 tablespoons of flour. Mix once more until the flour disappears, ensuring that no potato pieces are stuck together, then add the chopped pepper and briefly stir in. Place in the air fryer basket and air fry for 15–20 minutes until browned at the edges, turning them over halfway through.

Meanwhile, place the 6 tablespoons of flour in a medium bowl. Coat the chicken strips in the flour, one at a time, then squeeze them all at once to compact the flour onto them.

Transfer the cooked potato and pepper to a large baking tray, then keep warm in a low oven (or rewarm in the air fryer for 2 minutes once the chicken is done). Generously grease the base of the air fryer basket or crisping tray by spraying it with oil.

Add as many of the chicken strips as will fit into the air fryer without touching and spray with oil until the flour disappears. Air fry for 10 minutes until crisp, turning them halfway through.

Meanwhile, combine the spice mix ingredients in a small dish.

Once the chicken is done, add it to the baking tray with the chips (fries) and red pepper, then drizzle over the garlic-infused oil. Use a teaspoon to sprinkle half the spice mix on top, stir well until everything is coated, then repeat with the rest of the spice mix. Top with the spring onion greens and serve.

# SINGAPORE NOODLE 'STIR FRY'

 Use a low FODMAP curry powder.

 Replace the chicken and prawns (shrimp) with 250g (9oz) mushrooms, thinly sliced, adding them along with the (bell) pepper.

 Once cooked and cooled, freeze for up to 3 months. Allow to defrost in the fridge, then reheat in the microwave at 900W for 4–5 minutes. Check internal temp of the chicken with a digital food thermometer against those given on page 30.

- 2 large eggs
- 1 large red or green (bell) pepper, deseeded and chopped into thin strips
- 1 skinless chicken breast fillet, thinly sliced
- 1 tbsp garlic-infused oil
- Big handful of beansprouts
- 300g (10½oz) fresh vermicelli rice noodles
- 100g (3½oz) pre-cooked king prawns (jumbo shrimp)
- Handful of spring onion (scallion) greens or chives, finely chopped
- ½ tsp dried chilli flakes, to serve

**For the seasoning mix**
- 3 tsp gluten-free soy sauce
- 1 tsp mild curry powder
- ½ tsp ground turmeric
- ½ tsp ginger paste
- 1 tsp caster (superfine) sugar
- 2 tbsp garlic-infused oil
- ¼ tsp salt

**Serves 2–3 / Takes 20 minutes**

**A stir fry without a wok? While it might seem like a crazy idea, I promise that nobody would ever know you made this in the air fryer! Expect the same mildly spicy, curry-tinged noodles, packed with prawns and chicken, but with a method that doesn't really feel like you're cooking from scratch at all.**

Heat or preheat the air fryer to 200°C/400°F. Mix together the ingredients for the seasoning in a small bowl and set aside.

Crack each egg into two small ovenproof ramekins, beat and air fry for 6–7 minutes, mixing halfway through. Scramble each with a fork to break up the egg, then set aside. If you have an air fryer with two drawers, you can do this part in conjunction with the next step.

Add the sliced pepper and chicken to the air fryer basket or crisping tray, drizzle with the garlic-infused oil and stir until everything is well coated. Air fry for 7–8 minutes until the peppers are a little softened.

Add the beansprouts, rice noodles, prawns, scrambled egg chunks and the seasoning mix, then toss until everything is evenly dispersed. Air fry for a further 8 minutes, turning everything halfway through, until drier and a little crisp in places.

Finish with spring onion greens or chives and a sprinkle of chilli flakes. Serve alongside prawn crackers and your favourite Chinese fakeaway sides, like my prawn toast (page 162), egg-fried rice (page 165) or cheeseburger spring rolls (page 166).

## TIP

Wet noodles are most definitely not what you want in a dish like this! Adding the beansprouts, rice noodles and prawns introduces a lot of moisture, so if your noodles are still looking a little wet after air frying for 8 minutes, simply turn everything over once more and air fry for a few minutes longer. This recipe uses fresh, ready-to-fry rice noodles that you can buy in supermarkets. However, if you're using dried rice noodles, simply cook them first according to the packet instructions, then proceed with the recipe. About 100g (3½oz) of dried rice noodles should equate to 300g (10½oz) of cooked, fresh rice noodles.

# SHREDDED DUCK CHOW MEIN

 Once cooked and cooled, freeze for up to 3 months. Allow to defrost in the fridge, then reheat in the microwave at 900W for 4-5 minutes. Check internal temp of the duck with a digital food thermometer against those given on page 30.

- 450g (1lb) duck legs, bone in, skin on
- 2 tsp Chinese five spice powder
- 1 tsp ground ginger
- 2 medium carrots, thinly sliced on the diagonal
- 200g (7oz) dried ribbon rice noodles
- 5 tbsp gluten-free soy sauce
- 2 tsp sesame oil
- 1½ tbsp dark brown sugar
- Handful of beansprouts
- 2 handfuls of spring onion (scallion) greens, chopped

**Serves 2–3 / Takes 45 minutes**

**Though this might not seem like the fastest fakeaway in the world, the air fryer actually cuts down the time it takes to roast the duck legs by almost half, yet yields even crisper results! With duck-fat roasted carrots and crispy noodles, this might just be the best chow mein I've ever eaten.**

Pat the duck legs dry using kitchen paper, prick the skin all over with a skewer, then rub the five spice and ginger all over on both sides until completely and consistently covered.

Heat or preheat the air fryer to 180°C/350°F. Place the duck in the air fryer (basket or crisping tray in place), slightly spaced apart, and air fry for 25 minutes, turning twice throughout the cooking time, or until the skin is crisp. Remove to a wooden board and allow to rest for 10 minutes.

While the duck is resting, remove the crisping tray or basket from the air fryer (be careful as it will be hot!) and set the air fryer to 180°C/350°F again. Add the carrots to the duck juices in the bottom of the air fryer drawer, mix well, then air fry for 15 minutes, turning them halfway through.

Prepare the rice noodles according to the packet instructions – I briefly boil mine for 3–4 minutes, then drain. Once the duck has rested, remove and shred all of the meat and tear up the crispy skin using 2 forks.

Add the rice noodles, soy sauce, sesame oil and sugar to the air fryer with the carrots and toss everything until well coated.

Set the air fryer to 200°C/400°F. Air fry for 8 minutes, turning everything over halfway through, until the noodles are a little crispy on top. Add the beansprouts on top in a flat layer, then add the shredded duck on top and air fry for a further 5 minutes.

Toss well, then serve garnished with the spring onion greens alongside prawn toasts (page 162) and/or prawn crackers.

# SPEEDY CRISPY CHILLI BEEF

 Use oyster mushrooms (separated into very thin strands) instead of beef.

 See veggie advice.

 Once cooked and cooled, ideally freeze the beef strips and sauce separately for up to 3 months. Air fry the beef from frozen at 180°C/350°F for 5–6 minutes. Check internal temp with a digital food thermometer against those given on page 30. Reheat the sauce in the microwave at 360W, stirring every 3 minutes until piping hot.

- Vegetable oil in a spray bottle, for greasing
- 1 red (bell) pepper, deseeded and cut into 1cm (½ inch) chunks
- 50g (6 tbsp) gluten-free plain (all-purpose) flour
- 1 tsp salt
- 250g (9oz) beef sirloin steak, sliced into very thin strips

**For the sauce**
- 100ml (generous ⅓ cup) rice wine vinegar
- 2 tbsp garlic-infused oil
- 150g (¾ cup) caster (superfine) sugar
- 1 tsp dried chilli flakes
- 2 tbsp gluten-free soy sauce
- 3 tbsp water
- 2 tsp cornflour (cornstarch)

Serves 3 / Takes 25 minutes

**Meet the super-speedy, super-lazy air-fried version of a takeaway classic that uses a boatload less oil, but still results in crispy chilli beef that anyone would believe was just delivered to the door. Even the sweet, mildly spicy and sticky sauce can be made in around 5 minutes! Oh, and if you like it extra spicy, add an extra ½ teaspoon of chilli flakes.**

Heat or preheat the air fryer to 200°C/400°F. Lightly grease the base of the air fryer basket or crisping tray by spraying it with oil.

Add the red pepper and air fry for 10–12 minutes until slightly blackened in places.

Place the flour in a large bowl and stir in the salt. Dredge each individual piece of beef in the flour (leaving it in the bowl) and repeat until all the beef is coated.

Remove the cooked pepper from the air fryer to a plate and generously spray the basket once more with oil. Add as many of the beef strips as will comfortably fit into the air fryer without touching, and spray with oil until the flour disappears. Air fry for 10 minutes until crisp and a little golden brown at the edges, turning them over halfway through.

Meanwhile, add the vinegar, garlic-infused oil, sugar, dried chilli flakes and soy sauce to a medium saucepan and bring to the boil. Put the water and cornflour in a small dish and mix well. Once the sauce is boiling, add the cornflour mixture, stirring, and continue to boil for 2 minutes. Remove from the heat and allow to thicken and cool for 10 minutes.

Once the beef is done, add it to the saucepan, along with the red pepper (you might need to briefly rewarm in the air fryer for 2 minutes before adding). Mix and serve immediately with egg-fried rice (page 165) and prawn toasts (page 161).

**TIP**

Don't get rice wine vinegar confused with Chinese or Shaoxing rice wine, which not only isn't vinegar, but also contains gluten!

# CHICKEN OR STEAK FAJITAS

 Serve with dairy-free sour cream and dairy-free cheese.

 Serve with lactose-free sour cream.

 Serve with no more than 40g (1½oz) sour cream and 60g (2¼oz) avocado per person. Use all green (bell) peppers instead of red/yellow; ensure the chopped weight doesn't exceed 300g (10½oz).

 Follow the method for chicken fajitas and replace the chicken with a drained 400g (14oz) can of black beans, adding them for the final 5 minutes of cooking time.

 Combine the dairy-free and veggie advice.

 Once cooked and cooled, freeze for up to 3 months. Air fry from frozen at 180°C/350°F for 7-8 minutes. Check internal temp of the chicken or beef with a digital food thermometer against those given on page 30.

## For the fajita filling

- 400–500g (14-17oz) skinless chicken breast fillets, cut into thin strips **OR** 2 whole sirloin steaks, each 230-250g (8¼-9oz), fat trimmed
- 3 small red/green/yellow (bell) peppers, deseeded and cut into thin strips
- 1 tbsp garlic-infused oil
- ½ tsp cayenne pepper
- 2 tsp ground cumin
- 3 tsp dried oregano
- 2 tbsp smoked paprika
- 1 tsp salt

## To serve

- 2 medium avocados, mashed
- Store-bought mild or hot salsa
- 100g (3½oz) Cheddar, grated
- 150ml (⅝ cup) sour cream, topped with chopped chives
- 12 gluten-free wraps

**Serves 4 / Takes 20 minutes**

**Thanks to our air fryer, fajita night has quickly become our go-to, low-effort dinner that tastes way better than anything we could ever dream of ordering. By air frying the fajita filling instead of frying it like we usually would, you get a wonderful, slightly charred finish that matches how I've had them served in my favourite Mexican-style restaurants in the past. Bear in mind that if your sirloin steak is super thick or thin it may cook slower or faster than the timings provided.**

Mix together all the ingredients for the fajita filling in a large bowl so everything is well coated.

Heat or preheat the air fryer to 200°C/400°F.

If making chicken fajitas, place everything in the air fryer basket and air fry for 14–15 minutes, shaking the drawer halfway through to ensure everything cooks evenly.

If making steak fajitas, remove the coated steaks from the bowl and air fry for 10–12 minutes, turning them halfway through, for a medium finish. Air fry 2 minutes less for medium-rare or 2 minutes longer for well done. If you have a single-drawer air fryer, once the steak is done, transfer to a wooden board and allow to rest, then add the coated peppers to the drawer and air fry for 10–12 minutes until lightly blackened in places, turning them over halfway through. If you have a two drawer air fryer, simply cook the peppers in the second drawer while the steak is cooking. Allow the steaks to rest for at least 4–5 minutes before slicing into thin strips and mixing with the cooked peppers.

Serve with avocado, salsa, cheese, sour cream and wraps.

## TIP

You could swap one of the (bell) peppers for a small red onion (diced) if you'd prefer.

# NOTDONALD'S CHICKEN NUGGETS

 Omit the onion and garlic powders.

 Once cooked and cooled, freeze for up to 3 months. Air fry from frozen at 200°C/400°F for 6-7 minutes. Check internal temp with a digital food thermometer against those given on page 30.

- 400g (14oz) chicken breast mini fillets
- 40g (⅓ cup) cornflour (cornstarch)
- 1 large egg
- 100g (¾ cup) gluten-free plain (all-purpose) flour
- 30g (½ cup) gluten-free breadcrumbs (page 24)
- ¾ tsp celery salt
- ¼ tsp ground white pepper
- ¼ tsp ground black pepper
- ¼ tsp gluten-free baking powder
- ¼ tsp onion powder (optional)
- ¼ tsp garlic powder (optional)
- Pinch of ground turmeric (optional)
- Vegetable oil in a spray bottle, for greasing

**Here's my take on the famous chicken nugget, which first featured in my third book, *How to Plan Anything Gluten Free*, now adapted for air frying. Stick to the spice blend listed below for nuggets you won't believe aren't actually from the golden arches restaurant itself!**

Prepare the chicken by placing all the mini fillets on a chopping board, covering with cling film (plastic wrap) and bashing any thicker mini fillets until they are all about 1cm (½ inch) thick. Though this part is essentially optional, it helps to ensure even, faster cooking and more authentic nugget shapes!

Chop each mini fillet in half widthways to create 2 chicken nugget shapes.

Spread the cornflour out on a dinner plate. Beat the egg in a small bowl with a fork. Add the flour, breadcrumbs, celery salt, white and black pepper and baking powder, and the onion powder, garlic powder and turmeric if using, to a large bowl. Mix until everything is evenly dispersed.

Take 5 pieces of chicken at a time and roll them around in the plate of cornflour until well coated. Next, dip into the beaten egg bowl until coated once again. Finally, roll the chicken around in the seasoned flour and breadcrumbs until well covered with no eggy patches showing. Repeat until all your chicken pieces are coated.

Heat or preheat the air fryer to 200°C/400°F. Generously grease the base of the air fryer basket or crisping tray by spraying it with oil.

Add as many chicken pieces to the air fryer as will comfortably fit without touching, then spray generously with oil. Air fry for 10 minutes, turning them halfway through, until golden and crisp.

Serve with French fries (page 38) alongside your favourite dips.

# 'REAL DEAL' ZINGER BURGERS

 Use squares of dairy-free cheese instead of processed cheese.

 Use squares of Cheddar instead of processed cheese.

 Omit the onion and garlic powders. Serve with low FODMAP ketchup and squares of Cheddar instead of processed cheese.

 Use king oyster mushrooms, cut into 1cm (½ inch) thick slices, instead of chicken.

 Combine the dairy-free and veggie advice, then serve with vegan mayo.

 Once cooked and cooled, freeze for up to 3 months. Air fry from frozen at 180°C/350°F for 7–8 minutes. Check internal temp with a digital food thermometer against those given on page 30.

- 2 medium skinless chicken breast fillets (350g/12½oz in total)
- 1 large egg
- Vegetable oil in a spray bottle, for greasing

**For the spicy coating**
- 70g (generous ½ cup) gluten-free plain (all-purpose) flour
- 1 tsp gluten-free baking powder
- ½ tsp celery salt
- ½ tbsp smoked paprika
- ¼ tsp ground ginger
- ½ tsp cayenne pepper
- ½ tsp onion powder (optional)
- ½ tsp garlic powder (optional)

**To serve**
- 2 gluten-free burger buns, split
- 2 tsp mayonnaise
- Small handful of shredded lettuce
- 2 squares of processed cheese
- 2 tsp tomato ketchup

**Serves 2 / Takes 20 minutes**

Yes, Colonel Excell is back to recreate yet another fried chicken fakeaway – this time a certain crispy, spicy chicken burger you've probably been dreaming of since gluten departed from your life. As I ate this for the first time, I couldn't believe that a) this was gluten-free, b) I wasn't sitting in a fast-food restaurant, and c) this wasn't deep-fried and had in fact come out of my air fryer. Try it and see if you feel the same! (Pictured overleaf.)

To prepare the chicken breasts, butterfly them carefully using a large, sharp knife: lay them flat and slice horizontally so you can open each like a book, being careful not to cut all the way through! If you're not familiar with this technique (you could search online), you can always place the chicken breasts between 2 sheets of cling film (plastic wrap) and bash until flat with a rolling pin or meat mallet. Either way, we're aiming to make the chicken as flat as possible so it'll get more of that crispy coating and cook twice as fast.

Add the spicy coating ingredients to a medium bowl and mix until well combined. Beat the egg in a small bowl with a fork.

Dredge the chicken in the spicy coating bowl until well coated. Next, dip into the beaten egg until coated once again. Finally, roll the chicken around in the spicy coating bowl once more until well covered with no eggy patches showing.

Heat or preheat the air fryer to 200°C/400°F. Generously grease the base of the air fryer basket or crisping tray by spraying it with oil.

Place the prepared chicken in the air fryer basket and spray generously with oil until the floury patches disappear. Make sure the chicken fillets are touching as little as possible (or air fry in separate air fryer drawers if space is lacking).

Air fry for 8–10 minutes until the coating is crisp and golden, turning the fillets over halfway through and spraying lightly with oil once more.

Lightly toast the buns in the air fryer for 2–3 minutes until the bottoms and tops are a little crisp, but the bread inside still feels squidgy.

To construct, spread a thin layer of mayonnaise on the base of each bun, then top with shredded lettuce. Place a chicken fillet on next and top with a slice of processed cheese. Spread a thin layer of ketchup on the cut side of the top bun half, and place on top.

Serve with air fried fries (page 38) or sweet potato fries (page 41).

## TIPS

For a proper deep-fried finish, don't be afraid to be generous when spraying the chicken fillets with oil – spray them until it looks like the flour has vanished and you can actually see the chicken breast beneath. Conversely, if you want to use as little oil as possible, simply spray until there are no more white patches of flour visible; dry patches of flour will never turn golden and will burn, so make sure you spray just enough oil to prevent that.

Fancy making zinger-style air fried chicken, but without the bun? Simply use the spicy coating measurements to coat either chicken breast mini fillets or chicken thighs/drumstucks on the bone (skin on is fine) as described in the method to the left. If the weight of chicken you're using is more than specified in the recipe, simply double or triple the quantities of the spicy coating and the amount of eggs as required. Mini fillets will cook in 8-9 minutes at 200°C/400°F and chicken thighs/drumsticks on the bone will take 15-16 minutes – ensure you turn them over halfway and spray well with oil. Once they're looking done, you can always check the internal temperature with a digital food thermometer against those on page 30, to ensure they're cooked properly.

# LOADED CAJUN CHICKEN OR TOFU NACHOS

 Use a smoked dairy-free cheese that melts well instead of mozzarella.

 Use extra-firm tofu instead of chicken.

 Combine the dairy-free and veggie advice.

- 400g (14oz) chicken breast mini fillets, chopped into 2.5cm (1 inch) chunks **OR** 400g (14oz) extra-firm tofu, cut into 2.5cm (1 inch) chunks and coated in 50g (scant ½ cup) cornflour (cornstarch)
- 1 small red and 1 small green (bell) pepper, chopped into 5mm (¼ inch) strips
- 2 tbsp garlic-infused oil
- ½ tsp cayenne pepper
- 2 tsp ground cumin
- 1 tbsp dried oregano
- 1 tbsp smoked paprika
- 1 tsp salt
- 400g (14oz) gluten-free salted tortilla chips
- 125g (4½oz) mozzarella, grated
- 1 extra-large avocado, mashed with a pinch each of salt and ground black pepper
- ½ small jar of salsa
- Small handful of spring onion (scallion) greens, finely chopped

**Serves 3–4 / Takes 25 minutes**

**When you don't feel like biting into crispy tacos and having all the filling fall out of the back before your tongue even touches it, make my loaded nachos instead. Packed with juicy, mildly spicy Cajun chicken or tofu and charred (bell) peppers, topped with cheese and served with all the trimmings – this is the ultimate lazy version of 'Taco Tuesdays' that you'll crave every week!**

Mix the chicken **OR** cornflour-coated tofu with the peppers, garlic-infused oil, cayenne pepper, cumin, oregano, paprika and salt in a large bowl so everything is well coated.

Heat or preheat the air fryer to 200°C/400°F. Place the chicken/tofu in the air fryer basket and air fry for 12–13 minutes, turning everything over halfway through. Remove the cooked chicken/tofu and peppers to a (clean) bowl and add the tortilla chips to the air fryer.

Air fry for 2 minutes, or until the tortilla chips have turned from yellow to more of a golden brown, then turn them over. Add the chicken/tofu and peppers back in on top of the tortilla chips and spread out to a flat, even layer, then top with grated mozzarella. Air fry for a further 4 minutes or until the cheese is golden brown.

Transfer to a serving plate, then use an ice cream scoop to dollop the mashed avocado around in places. Top with spoonfuls of salsa, sprinkle over the spring onion greens, then dig in.

## TIP

Don't let the tortilla chips get too dark – ensure you keep an eye on them! If you put fewer chips in the drawer or have a very large air fryer, they might cook more quickly than the timings stated.

# 20-MINUTE PIZZA

 Use a thick dairy-free yoghurt and dairy-free cheese.

 Use lactose-free Greek yoghurt.

 Use lactose-free Greek yoghurt and a low FODMAP BBQ sauce, if using.

 Use veggie-friendly toppings.

 See dairy-free advice and use vegan-friendly toppings.

 Once cooked and cooled, freeze for up to 3 months. Air fry from frozen at 180°C/350°F for 9–10 minutes.

- Large handful of grated mozzarella
- Toppings of your choice, such as pepperoni, tuna, thinly sliced (bell) peppers, ham and pineapple
- Large handful of rocket (arugula), to serve (optional)

### For the base
- 220g (1⅘ cups) gluten-free self-raising flour, plus extra for dusting
- 110g (½ cup) Greek yoghurt (or thick natural yoghurt)
- 75ml (scant ⅓ cup) water
- 1 tbsp dried mixed herbs
- 1 tsp salt

### For the sauce
- 150ml (⅝ cup) tomato passata
- 1 tsp garlic-infused oil
- 1 tsp dried mixed herbs
- 1 tbsp gluten-free BBQ sauce (optional; for a BBQ base)
- Pinch each of salt and ground black pepper

**Makes three 18cm (7 inch) pizzas / Takes 20 minutes**

**Did you know that air fryers are also amazing mini pizza ovens? Expect a crisper base and a restaurant-like finish to your toppings every time when compared to using an oven. The number of pizzas you can make (and their size) depends on how big your air fryer basket is – the size of my air fryer drawers (15 x 20cm/6 x 8 inches) allow me to make 3 rectangular pizzas out of the dough quantity given, which is enough to serve 2 people with a side of rocket (arugula). But if your air fryer basket is larger than mine, feel free to make 2 larger pizzas.**

Add the base ingredients to a large bowl, giving the yoghurt a good stir before adding. Mix thoroughly using a spatula to ensure there are no hidden clumps of yoghurt-coated flour. As it starts to come together, use your hands to bring it together into a slightly sticky ball.

Knead the dough briefly in the bowl until smooth, combined and no longer sticky. Dough still too sticky? Add a little more flour. Dough too dry? Add a little more water.

Transfer the dough to a sheet of non-stick baking parchment that's comfortably larger than your air fryer basket or crisping tray. Cut the dough into 3 equal portions.

Lightly flour a rolling pin and roll out one of the dough portions (place the other 2 back in the bowl and cover) so it either matches the shape of your air fryer basket or crisping tray (usually either a rectangle or a circle) or is slightly smaller. Roll until about 3mm (⅛ inch) thick, ensuring the dough is nice and even and not thicker or thinner in certain areas. Re-flour the rolling pin as necessary to stop it from sticking. Form a raised border around the dough by gently rolling the edges inwards a little, then trim the baking parchment around the pizza base. Repeat with the other dough portions on separate sheets of baking parchment.

**continued overleaf**

For the sauce, combine all the ingredients in a small bowl. Spread about 2 tablespoons of sauce onto each base, right up to the border. Use the baking parchment to lift one of the pizza bases into the air fryer basket (you can cook two at a time if you have more than one air fryer drawer). Add some mozzarella, followed by the toppings of your choice, pressing any lighter toppings like pepperoni in a little, or else they might fly about in the air fryer!

Heat or preheat the air fryer to 200°C/400°F and air fry for 7 minutes, or until the mozzarella is golden and the toppings are nicely seared. Air fry any remaining pizzas until they're done. Remove using a spatula and serve with rocket, if you like.

## TIP

The key to a crisp base is to first of all ensure the dough is rolled as thinly as possible. Secondly, don't overload each base with sauce and toppings, as this can make the base more 'bready' than crisp.

# CHICKEN BALTI POT PIES

 **DF** Use a thick dairy-free yoghurt.

 **LF** Use lactose-free Greek yoghurt.

 **V** Use a 400g (14oz) can of drained chickpeas instead of chicken.

 **VE** Combine the dairy-free and veggie advice and use sweetened almond milk instead of egg to brush the pastry.

 Once cooked and cooled, freeze for up to 3 months. Allow to defrost in the fridge, then air fry at 180°C/350°F for 8–9 minutes. Check internal temp with a digital food thermometer against those given on page 30.

- 1 small onion or 1 medium carrot, peeled and cut into 5mm (¼ inch) dice
- 1 medium potato, peeled and cut into 5mm (¼ inch) dice
- 250–300g (9–10½oz) skinless, boneless chicken thighs, cut into small strips, about 2cm (¾ inch) long and 1cm (½ inch) wide
- 1 tbsp garlic-infused oil
- 1 tsp mild curry powder
- ½ tsp garam masala, plus an extra ½ tsp for the sauce
- 1 tsp dried chilli flakes or Kashmiri chilli flakes
- Vegetable oil in a spray bottle, for greasing
- 280g (10oz) store-bought ready-rolled gluten-free puff pastry
- 250ml (1 cup) tomato passata
- ½ tsp salt
- 1 tsp ginger paste
- Handful of spinach, chopped
- 1 tbsp mango chutney
- 2 heaped tbsp Greek yoghurt
- 1 small egg, beaten

**Makes 2 / Takes 30 minutes**

**These pastry-topped, golden pot pies with a creamy, mildly spicy chicken curry filling are a familiar favourite at football grounds all across the UK... but apparently enjoying football and being gluten-free are two things that can't occur simultaneously! Yep, sadly they're never ever gluten-free, so instead I make my own at home and enjoy them in front of football on the telly. Who knows? Maybe one day I can get Ipswich Town FC to sell a version of these at Portman road!**

Add the onion or carrot, potato, chicken, garlic-infused oil, curry powder, garam masala and chilli flakes to a large bowl, then mix well until everything is well coated in the spices.

Heat or preheat the air fryer to 200°C/400°F. Lightly grease the base of the air fryer basket or crisping tray by spraying it with a little oil.

Add the coated chicken and veg to the air fryer and spread out into an even layer. Air fry for 15 minutes or until the chicken is golden brown, turning everything over halfway through.

Meanwhile, remove the pastry from the fridge – this makes it easier to unroll without breaking or cracking it.

Place the passata, salt and ginger in a small saucepan and briefly mix. Place over a medium heat, add the spinach and simmer until the spinach has wilted, then stir. Mix in the mango chutney and yoghurt and simmer until the sauce has thickened a little, which should be roughly when the chicken and veg is ready in the air fryer. Stir in the extra ½ teaspoon of garam masala to finish the sauce.

Add the chicken and veg to the sauce and stir in until well coated, then remove from the heat and allow to cool briefly. Have ready two 15cm (6 inch) rectangular or circular pie dishes that will comfortably fit into your air fryer.

Unroll the sheet of puff pastry, and use the pie dishes as a guide to cut out 2 pastry lids that are 1cm (½ inch) larger than the the dish – use a small, sharp knife for this.

**continued overleaf**

Once the filling has cooled a little, divide it between the pie dishes and flatten down gently into an even layer. Brush the brim of the dish all the way around with some of the beaten egg and place a pastry lid on top of each pie dish, gently pressing down at the edges – ensure that the pastry overhangs the edges and press the overhang against the side of the dish.

Use a small, sharp knife to score a criss-cross pattern on top of the pastry (don't cut through it!) and brush all over with more beaten egg.

Place in the air fryer and air fry at 200°C/400°F for 7–8 minutes or until the pastry is golden and crisp on top.

Serve with mashed potato, spicy potato wedges (page 38) or sweet potato wedges (page 41) and steamed spring greens or air fried veggies of your choice (page 175). I like to have mango chutney on the side for dipping too!

## TIPS

Save any leftover passata for my air fryer pizzas (page 144), crispy parmesan chicken (page 82) or calzone (page 100), or use in place of chopped tomatoes in your favourite pasta dishes.

You can easily use the construction method, temperature and timings given here to air fry different pie fillings that you'll find in my other books. Simply prepare the filling from the recipe of your choice, then use it to make as many pot-pies as the filling and pastry will allow.

# CHICKEN SHAWARMA KEBABS

 Once cooked and cooled, freeze for up to 3 months. Air fry from frozen at 180°C/350°F for 5-6 minutes. Check internal temp with a digital food thermometer against those given on page 30.

- 650g (1lb 7oz) chicken breast mini fillets
- Vegetable oil in a spray bottle, for greasing
- Small handful of coriander (cilantro), roughly chopped
- Side salad of your choice

**For the marinade**

- 1-2 tbsp lemon juice
- 2 tsp smoked paprika
- 1 tsp ground coriander
- 1 tsp ground cumin
- ½ tsp cayenne pepper
- 1 tsp salt

Makes 8 / Takes 20 minutes + (optional) marinating

**Here's the perfect answer to the question, 'What should I cook with this chicken in the fridge?' Expect tender chicken with an almost BBQ-like slightly charred finish and a whirlwind of spices that'll go down a storm, especially when served with flatbreads. Chicken mini fillets mean there's no chopping required, but feel free to use whole chicken breast fillets cut into 2.5cm (1 inch) cubes too.**

Combine the marinade ingredients in a large bowl. Add the chicken and mix until well coated. Optionally cover and transfer to the fridge to marinate for 30 minutes and up to 4 hours.

Grab 8 wooden or metal skewers – most importantly, they need to fit into your air fryer, so check that they do first. Wooden skewers can be trimmed to fit. Thread 2 mini fillets onto each skewer.

Heat or preheat the air fryer to 200°C/400°F. Generously grease the base of the air fryer basket or crisping tray by spraying it with oil.

Place as many skewers as will fit into the air fryer at once without touching, and lightly spray with oil. Air fry for 12–14 minutes, turning them halfway through, until the chicken is a little blackened at the edges.

Sprinkle over the coriander and serve with store-bought gluten-free pitta breads or my mozzarella-stuffed flatbreads (page 186), a side salad of your choice, and mayo mixed with a dash of chilli oil, if you like.

# DONER KEBABS

 Once cooked, cooled and shaved, freeze for up to 3 months. Air fry from frozen at 180°C/350°F for 5-6 minutes. Check internal temp with a digital food thermometer against those given on page 30.

**For the kebab**
- 250g (9oz) minced (ground) lamb
- 250g (9oz) minced (ground) beef
- 1 tsp ground cumin
- 1 tsp smoked paprika
- 1 tsp ground coriander
- 1 tbsp dried mixed herbs
- 3 tbsp garlic-infused oil
- 1 large egg
- 1 tsp salt
- ¼ tsp ground black pepper

**For the herby garlic dip (optional)**
- 100ml (generous ⅓ cup) mayonnaise
- 1½ tsp garlic-infused olive oil
- 1½ tsp dried mixed herbs

**Serves 4 / Takes 50 minutes**

**This homemade doner kebab is famous in our house, not just because of how juicy and succulent the meat is, but also because of how such a low amount of effort could ever yield such rewarding results!**

If using a food processor or a large blender, add all the kebab ingredients to it and process until smooth. (To mix by hand, add everything to a large bowl and mix with a wooden spoon until everything is super-smooth and there's no more texture visible in the mince.) The smoother your mince is, the more likely you'll be able to shave off larger pieces when it's cooked.

Have ready a large sheet of foil and, with the longer side of the foil closest to you, place the kebab mixture on the foil in front of you, a few inches away from the edge. Form it into a rough sausage shape, then, using the foil, tightly roll it away from you. Bunch together the open ends of the foil and twist them simultaneously to tightly seal. You should be left with a tightly wrapped foil-coated sausage shape (with no tears in the foil!) around 7.5 (3 inches) thick and 18cm (7 inches) long.

Heat or preheat the air fryer to 160°C/320°F. Place the wrapped kebab in the air fryer and air fry for 35 minutes. Remove to a plate and open the foil so that the meat is sitting in a 'bowl' of foil, then return to the air fryer. Air fry at 180°C/350°F for 6–7 minutes until browned, then turn it over and air fry for a further 5 minutes.

Allow to rest for 15–20 minutes if you have the time – that way, you'll get cleaner shavings off it. Meanwhile, mix together the ingredients for the dip, if serving, in a small dish.

Once the kebab has rested, take a sharp knife and shave off lots of super-thin slices.

Serve alongside the garlic and herb dip, if using, and store-bought gluten-free flatbreads or my stuffed flatbreads (page 186). I like to elevate my doner with cucumber ribbons, shredded lettuce, sliced tomatoes, red cabbage and pickled chillies.

# CHEESEBURGER CRUNCH QUESADILLAS

 Use a square slice of dairy-free cheese that melts well instead of processed cheese, and dairy-free sour cream.

 Use a square slice of Cheddar instead of processed cheese and use lactose-free sour cream.

 Once cooked and cooled, freeze for up to 3 months. Air fry from frozen at 180°C/350°F for 8–9 minutes. Check internal temp with a digital food thermometer against those given on page 30.

- 500g (1lb 2oz) lean minced (ground) beef (5% fat)
- 1 tbsp garlic-infused oil
- 1 tsp smoked paprika
- 1 tsp dried oregano
- 1 tsp ground cumin
- ½ tsp cayenne pepper
- Vegetable oil in a spray bottle, for greasing
- 6 gluten-free tortilla wraps, 15cm (6 inches) diameter
- 3 slices of processed cheese
- 2 small handfuls of gluten-free tortilla chips
- Small handful of iceberg lettuce, shredded
- 3-4 tsp fresh mild salsa (from a jar)
- 3-4 tsp sour cream

**To serve**
- 1 large avocado, mashed
- Burger sauce (ensure gluten-free)

**Serves 2 (makes 3) / Takes 20 minutes**

**Inspired by a certain Mexican-style fast-food chain's famous crunch wraps, these quesadillas feature mildly spicy beef and crispy tortilla chips, topped with all the trimmings and sandwiched between two crisp tortilla wraps. With a minor method amendment to ensure the tortilla wraps don't flap open in the air fryer (I make quesadilla 'sandwiches' instead of folding them over), this is a deceptively easy fakeaway to rustle up.**

Add the beef, garlic-infused oil, smoked paprika, oregano, cumin and cayenne pepper to a large bowl, then stir well until the beef is well coated.

Heat or preheat the air fryer to 180°C/350°F. Lightly grease the base of the air fryer basket or crisping tray by spraying it with oil.

Add the beef to the air fryer and air fry for 6–7 minutes, turning it over halfway through, until browned.

Have ready a tortilla wrap and top with a few tablespoons of minced beef in an even layer, leaving a 2cm (¾ inch) clear border around the edges. Top with a slice of cheese, 3–4 tortilla chips, some shredded lettuce and small dollops of salsa. Spread a thin layer of sour cream on another tortilla and sandwich it on top, gently applying pressure to flatten the filling. Repeat with the rest of the beef, toppings and tortilla wraps.

Generously grease the base of the air fryer if there isn't much left after air frying the beef. Add as many of the tortilla sandwiches to the air fryer as will comfortably fit without touching, and lightly spray with oil. Air fry for 6–7 minutes, or until the tortilla is browned and crispy on top, then remove from the air fryer.

Use a sharp knife to slice each in half or quarters, and serve with a side of mashed avocado and burger sauce as a dip.

# STARTERS, SIDES & SNACKS

Not surprisingly, all my favourite starters, sides and savoury snacks are more often than not coated in a layer of crispy breadcrumbs, batter or golden pastry. And this was true long before I was gluten-free – it's not just because I can no longer eat them!

But since getting my air fryer, it's no surprise that all of my old favourites now feature on my dinner plate very regularly; not only are they easy to make gluten-free, and healthier because there's no need to deep-fry them anymore, they're so much faster to make with less washing up too.

So revel with me in the return of so many of our crispy, crunchy, golden favourites and enjoy them alongside the main courses in this book, or air fry a bunch of different sides from this chapter to create your own sharing platters or party-food spreads.

# PARMESAN CHICKEN TENDERS

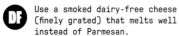
Use a smoked dairy-free cheese (finely grated) that melts well instead of Parmesan.

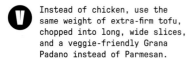
Instead of chicken, use the same weight of extra-firm tofu, chopped into long, wide slices, and a veggie-friendly Grana Padano instead of Parmesan.

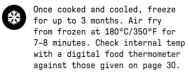
Once cooked and cooled, freeze for up to 3 months. Air fry from frozen at 180°C/350°F for 7-8 minutes. Check internal temp with a digital food thermometer against those given on page 30.

- 40g (⅓ cup) cornflour (cornstarch)
- 1 tsp smoked paprika
- 1 tsp dried mixed herbs
- ½ tsp each of salt and ground black pepper
- 1 large egg, beaten
- 80g (1⅓ cups) gluten-free breadcrumbs or 120g (4¼oz) crushed gluten-free cornflakes
- 40g (1½oz) Parmesan, grated
- 400g (14oz) chicken breast mini fillets
- Vegetable oil in a spray bottle, for greasing

**Serves 2-3 / Takes 20 minutes**

**The perfect golden, crunchy, cheesy chicken dippers are only ever 20 minutes away, thanks to this super-simple recipe, and you'd never know they weren't deep-fried. Chicken mini fillets are ideal for making chicken tenders as they're already the perfect shape with no chopping required – plus they cook extremely fast in the air fryer!**

Add the cornflour, smoked paprika, mixed herbs, salt and pepper to a medium bowl. Beat the egg in a small bowl with a fork. Spread the breadcrumbs or crushed cornflakes out on a dinner plate with the grated Parmesan, then briefly mix together.

Take one mini fillet at a time and roll around in the seasoned cornflour until well coated. Next, dip into the beaten egg bowl until coated once again. Finally, roll it around in the breadcrumbs or cornflakes until well covered with no eggy patches showing, gently squeezing and compacting the coating onto the chicken. Repeat until all the mini fillets are coated.

Heat or preheat the air fryer to 200°C/400°F. Generously grease the base of the air fryer basket or crisping tray by spraying it with oil.

Add as many chicken tenders to the air fryer as will comfortably fit without touching, then spray generously with oil. Air fry for 8–9 minutes, turning them halfway through, until golden and crisp.

Serve with fries (page 38) or loaded potato skins (page 178) alongside your favourite dips, or create a party food platter along with my cheeseburger spring rolls (page 166), prawn toast (page 162), onion rings (page 181) and halloumi popcorn (page 161).

# HALLOUMI POPCORN

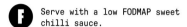

**F** Serve with a low FODMAP sweet chilli sauce.

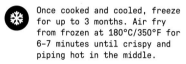 Once cooked and cooled, freeze for up to 3 months. Air fry from frozen at 180°C/350°F for 6-7 minutes until crispy and piping hot in the middle.

- 225g (8oz) halloumi
- 1 large egg
- Pinch each of salt and pepper
- 5 tbsp gluten-free plain (all-purpose) flour or cornflour (cornstarch)
- 5 tbsp gluten-free breadcrumbs (page 24)
- 1 tsp smoked paprika
- Vegetable oil in a spray bottle, for greasing
- Sweet chilli sauce (ensure gluten-free), to serve

**Serves 2-3 / Takes 15 minutes**

**Social media is a strange place for someone like me, who can spend two days working on a recipe video that achieves a resounding tumbleweed, or 15 minutes on this recipe, which netted 1.5 million views across Instagram and TikTok. Either way, it doesn't change the fact that halloumi in a crispy coating is incredibly moreish, and you should probably make this for that reason alone.**

To prepare the halloumi, firmly pat it dry with kitchen paper if it's particularly wet, then cut it into 2cm (¾ inch) cubes.

Using a fork, beat the egg in a small bowl with the salt and pepper added. Spread the flour out on a large dinner plate, then spread the breadcrumbs and paprika out on another large dinner plate and mix together.

Take the halloumi cubes and dredge in the flour until lightly dusted on all sides. Then one by one dip them into the beaten egg until coated once again. Next, roll in the breadcrumbs until tightly covered on all sides.

Heat or preheat the air fryer to 200°C/400°F. Generously grease the base of the air fryer basket or crisping tray by spraying it with oil. Place in the air fryer basket, spray generously with oil and air fry for 8-10 minutes until golden, turning them over halfway through.

Serve as party food canapés with sweet chilli sauce for dipping, or for lunch in a salad with a drizzle of sweet chilli sauce.

# PRAWN TOAST

 Serve with a low FODMAP sweet chilli sauce.

 Once cooked and cooled, freeze for up to 3 months. Air fry from frozen at 200°C/400°F for 5-8 minutes. Check internal temp with a digital food thermometer against those given on page 30.

- 165g (6oz) raw peeled prawns (shrimp), deveined
- 1 tsp ginger paste
- ¼ tsp caster (superfine) sugar
- Pinch of salt
- ¼ tsp ground black pepper
- 2 tbsp water
- 1 tbsp gluten-free soy sauce
- 6-9 slices of white gluten-free bread
- 70g (½ cup) sesame seeds
- Vegetable oil in a spray bottle, for greasing
- Sweet chilli sauce (ensure gluten-free), to serve

**Serves 6-7 (makes 24-36) / Takes 25 minutes**

**Without a doubt, this might be the healthiest recipe in this book when compared to the deep-fried version of this Chinese takeaway side dish. And that's simply because bread absorbs oil like a sponge when deep-fried! But in the air fryer, a few spritzes of oil goes a long way in achieving a golden, crispy finish because, after all, bread doesn't need tons of oil to turn into toast, does it?**

Place the prawns, ginger paste, sugar, salt, pepper, water and soy sauce in a food processor. Blitz until the mixture reaches a smooth, spreadable consistency. (If you don't have a food processor, use a sharp knife to chop the prawns into a smooth paste before combining them with the other ingredients in a large bowl.)

Spread the prawn mixture across each slice of bread and make sure you go right up to the edges. You should have enough for up to 9 slices of bread if you're economical with your spreading.

Spread the sesame seeds onto a dinner plate. Place the bread prawn-side down into the sesame seeds until fully covered. Repeat for all the slices of bread. Cut each topped slice of bread into 4 equal triangles.

Heat or preheat the air fryer to 200°C/400°F. Generously grease the base of the air fryer basket or crisping tray by spraying it with oil.

Add as many prawn toasts to the air fryer as will comfortably fit without touching, then generously spray with oil. Air fry for 6–7 minutes, until golden on both sides, turning them halfway through and spraying generously once more with oil.

Serve with sweet chilli dipping sauce, alongside Singapore noodles (page 129), sweet and sour chicken/pork (page 121), shredded duck chow mein (page 130) or egg-fried rice (page 165).

# TAKEAWAY-STYLE EGG-FRIED RICE

Use 100g (3½oz) crumbled extra-firm tofu mixed with a pinch of turmeric (to make it yellow) in place of the eggs.

- 500g (1lb 2oz) cooked long-grain rice, cooled and ideally chilled overnight, or 2 x 250g (9oz) packets of microwaveable long-grain rice
- 1 tbsp sesame oil
- 2 tbsp gluten-free soy sauce
- 2 large eggs
- Small handful of frozen peas
- Salt

**Serves 3 / Takes 15 minutes**

**This air fryer version of a Chinese takeaway staple is delicious whether you use a packet of microwaveable rice or leftover cooked rice (considerably cheaper than microwave rice!) from yesterday's dinner. Not only does it result in wonderful, crispy rice as though it were fried, but air frying it is also incredibly handy when you already have a wok on the go that's preparing your fakeaway main.**

Heat or preheat the air fryer to 200°C/400°F with the crisping tray or basket removed.

Add the rice, sesame oil and soy sauce to the air fryer and stir well until the rice is well coated. Air fry for 5 minutes, stirring and breaking up any lumps of rice halfway through, then create a large well in the rice by pushing all the rice to the sides of the air fryer. Crack in both eggs, season with a little salt and break the yolks.

Air fry for 5 more minutes, or until the egg is cooked, occassionally breaking up the egg and carefully turning any rice that seems like it's getting a little too crispy. If possible, avoid mixing the egg into the rice until it's cooked.

Once the egg is done, mix the rice and egg chunks together, then add the frozen peas on top, but don't mix them in yet. Air fry for a further 2–3 minutes or until you notice the rice is a little crispy in places. Stir in the peas.

Serve alongside your Chinese fakeaway favourites, like sweet and sour pork/chicken (page 121) or crispy chilli beef (page 133), or with my teriyaki salmon (page 62).

# CHEESEBURGER SPRING ROLLS

**DF** Use a smoked dairy-free cheese (grated) that melts well instead of processed cheese.

**LL** Use Monterey Jack cheese (grated) instead of processed cheese.

**F** Use Monterey Jack cheese (grated) instead of processed cheese.

**❄** Once cooked and cooled, freeze for up to 3 months. Air fry from frozen at 200°C/400°F for 7-9 minutes. Check internal temp with a digital food thermometer against those given on page 30.

- Vegetable oil in a spray bottle, for greasing
- 500g (1lb 2oz) lean minced (ground) beef (5% fat)
- ½ tsp salt
- ¼ tsp ground black pepper
- 100g (3½oz) gherkins, finely chopped
- 5 slices of processed cheese
- 50g (6 tbsp) gluten-free plain (all-purpose) flour
- About 200ml (scant ¾ cup) water
- 10 rice spring roll wrappers
- Burger sauce (ensure gluten-free), to serve

**Makes 10 / Takes 30 minutes**

**These beauties were inspired by the cheeseburger spring rolls at Disney World: minced (ground) beef, cheese and chopped gherkins all encased in a crispy shell. As I'll never be able to eat one in my lifetime, I used rice spring roll wrappers to recreate them at home – and I'm so glad I did! There are always rice spring roll wrappers in supermarkets (usually with all the other international cooking ingredients and sauces) but sometimes they're just called 'Vietnamese spring roll wrappers'.**

Heat or preheat the air fryer to 200°C/400°F. Lightly grease the base of the air fryer basket or crisping tray by spraying it with oil.

Add the beef to the air fryer, season with the salt and pepper, then break up the mince.

Air fry for 6–7 minutes, turning the beef over halfway through, until browned. Transfer to a large bowl, add the gherkins and processed cheese, then mix well with a wooden spoon until the processed cheese is broken up and evenly dispersed.

Next, construct the spring rolls. Spread the flour out on a large dinner plate. Add the water to a second large dinner plate (ensure the plate has a decent amount of depth and a lip at the edges to contain the water) so it's nice and shallow.

Take one sheet of rice paper and dip it in the water for 5 seconds, immersing it completely. Then place the wrapper on a suitably sized wooden board (or a damp cloth) where you'll roll your spring rolls.

After around 10–15 seconds, the rice paper should feel more flexible and slightly sticky.

Add 55g (2oz) of the beef filling to the rice wrapper just below the centre (about 4cm/1½ inches from the bottom) and mould it into a sausage shape with your hands. Fold the bottom of the rice wrapper so that it just overlaps the filling and roll forwards once. Fold in the left and right sides of the wrapper and continue to tightly roll up.

**continued overleaf**

Transfer to the flour plate and roll around until lightly dusted, then set aside. Repeat until you've made 10 spring rolls.

Heat or preheat the air fryer to 200°C/400°F. Generously grease the base of the air fryer if there isn't much oil left after air frying the beef. Add as many spring rolls as will comfortably fit without touching to the air fryer. Generously spray with oil and air fry for 15 minutes, turning them halfway through, until crisp all over.

Transfer to a wire rack and allow to cool for 5–10 minutes before serving. Serve alongside Singapore noodles (page 129), sweet and sour chicken/pork (page 121), shredded duck chow mein (page 130) and the burger sauce for dipping.

## TIP

Digital weighing scales can make portioning out exactly 55g (2oz) of the filling incredibly easy, ensuring that each spring roll is exactly the same size and that they all cook in the same time. Simply put the bowl containing the filling on the scale and press the 'zero' button to set the weight to zero. Once you remove the filling, the scale will show you how much you've removed, so you can continue to take it out until the scale reads -55g. For each spring roll, simply press the 'zero' button again and portion out once more. Try using this technique when you need to weigh out portions for other recipes and thank me later!

# BAKERY-STYLE SAUSAGE ROLLS OR VEGGIE BAKES

 Use a smoked dairy-free cheese that melts well and dairy-free cream cheese.

 Use lactose-free cream cheese.

 **Sausage rolls:** use FODMAP-friendly sausages.
**Bakes:** use lactose-free cream cheese and a mix of FODMAP-friendly veg, chopped into 5mm (¼ inch) chunks.

 Use gluten-free veggie-friendly sausages.

 Make the veggie bakes using the dairy-free advice and brush with unsweetened almond milk instead of egg.

 Once cooked and cooled, freeze for up to 3 months. Defrost fully in the fridge before reheating in the air fryer following the temps/timings in the recipe.

- 280g (10oz) store-bought ready-rolled gluten-free puff pastry, about 24 x 30cm (9½ x 12 inches)
- 1 large egg, beaten
- Vegetable oil in a spray bottle, for greasing

**For sausage rolls**
- 6 gluten-free sausages (about 400g/14oz total weight)

**For veggie bakes**
- 200g (7oz) store-bought mashed potato
- 50g (1¾oz) extra-mature Cheddar, grated
- 4 tbsp cream cheese
- 1 tsp salt
- ¼ tsp ground black pepper
- 150g (5½oz) frozen mixed veg, such as sweetcorn, peas, green beans and carrots
- 1 tbsp water

**Makes 4 rolls or 2 bakes / Takes 25 minutes**

**If you've been missing out on regular trips to a certain bakery chain to enjoy one of your favourite savoury snacks (like 99% of the rest of the population!) then this is most certainly the recipe for you. Either make four large sausage rolls or 2 large veggie bakes – the choice is yours.**

Remove the pastry from the fridge 10 minutes before starting – this makes it easier to unroll without breaking or cracking.

**To make sausage rolls:** Remove the sausages from their casing and discard the casing. Add the sausagemeat to a medium bowl and mix together until it forms a smooth paste.

Unroll the puff pastry on a flat work surface with a long side closest to you. Use a pizza cutter (I also use a long ruler to ensure I'm cutting straight) to cut horizontally, dividing the pastry into two equal strips. Arrange the sausagemeat in a long line down the length of the strips, leaving a large gap above and about a 1.25cm (½ inch) gap on the below edge. Compact it a little with your fingers so it's not so loose.

Brush the smaller edge of the pastry with beaten egg, then fold the larger side of the pastry over the sausagemeat. Using your fingers, gently form the pastry around the sausagemeat while compacting it to remove any gaps.

Crimp the pastry all along the seam using a fork to securely seal it shut. Use a large, sharp knife to cut into 4 large, long sausage rolls, then slash each sausage roll diagonally three times (ensuring you don't cut right through the pastry). Brush each sausage roll with beaten egg.

Heat or preheat the air fryer to 200°C/400°F. Lightly grease the base of the air fryer basket or crisping tray by spraying it with a little oil. Place as many sausage rolls as will fit into the air fryer without touching and air fry for 12–14 minutes until golden and crisp.

**continued overleaf**

**To make veggie bakes:** Place the mashed potato in a large microwave-safe bowl, cover and microwave for 2 minutes at full power (900W) until piping hot. Add the grated cheese, cream cheese, salt and pepper, then stir in and set aside.

Place the frozen mixed veg in a suitably sized, microwave-safe bowl and add the water. Loosely cover with a plate and microwave for 5 minutes on full power (900W) until completely cooked through. Drain and transfer to a chopping board, then use a sharp knife to chop up any larger pieces, ensuring they're all roughly the same size as any peas and sweetcorn. Transfer to the bowl of cheesy mash.

Unroll the puff pastry on a flat work surface. Cut in half vertically and horizontally so you have with 4 rectangles (I use a pizza cutter and a long ruler to ensure I'm cutting straight).

Spoon half the filling onto two of the rectangles, leaving a 1cm (½ inch) clear border all around the edge of the rectangle.

Brush beaten egg all around the edges and place the other pastry rectangles on top, gently pressing down to seal. Crimp the edges using a fork, then arrange both bakes in the middle of the baking parchment, with a 2.5cm (1 inch) gap between them. At this point, you're welcome to lightly score chevron-style lines in the top of the pastry using a small, sharp knife (ensuring you don't cut right through the pastry) for the ultimate finishing touch.

Heat or preheat the air fryer to 200°C/400°F. Lightly grease the base of the air fryer basket or crisping tray by spraying it with a little oil. Place as many veggie bakes as will fit into the air fryer without touching and air fry for 10–12 minutes until golden and crisp, then serve with ketchup or your favourite dip.

## TIPS

There's no need to keep the sausage rolls/veggie bakes on the baking parchment during cooking; simply discard it and place them into the air fryer without it.

You're welcome to make your own mashed potato, or use leftovers, but store-bought mash is convenient for this recipe.

# 4-INGREDIENT SCOTCH EGGS

Ensure sausages are FODMAP-friendly.

- 4 large eggs
- 6 gluten-free sausages (about 400g/14oz total weight)
- 25g (3 tbsp) gluten-free plain (all-purpose) flour
- 60g (1 cup) gluten-free breadcrumbs (page 24)
- Vegetable oil in a spray bottle, for greasing

**Makes 3 / Takes 30 minutes + cooling**

**Not only do I struggle to believe that these crispy, golden Scotch eggs came out of my air fryer and weren't pan/deep-fried, I still haven't come to terms with just how well an air fryer can churn out soft-boiled eggs. Yes, instead of boiling them, you simply just air fry them for a few minutes (see page 32 for specific timings), so please take away that knowledge from this recipe too, and use it to make dippy eggs and soldiers!**

Heat or preheat the air fryer to 150°C/300°F.

Place 3 of the eggs in the air fryer and air fry for 6–7 minutes (see TIP overleaf). Remove from the air fryer and allow to cool until cold enough to peel (about 10 minutes).

Meanwhile, remove the sausages from their casing and discard the casing. Add the sausagemeat to a medium bowl and mix together until it forms a smooth paste. Divide the sausagemeat into thirds that should weigh just over 130g (4¾oz) each, and then roll into balls.

Spread the flour over a dinner plate, crack the remaining egg into a small bowl and beat with a fork, then spread the breadcrumbs out on a second dinner plate.

Have ready a medium sheet of cling film (plastic wrap) and place a sausagemeat ball in the centre. Fold one side of the cling film over it and press it flat with your hands so that it's about five times longer than the boiled egg and twice as wide (assuming the egg is lying sideways).

Unfold the cling film so it's completely flat again and place a peeled egg on top. Slide your hand under the cling film so the meat and egg is in the palm of your hand, then use the cling film to shape the sausagemeat around the egg, ensuring the seam where it meets is gently compacted and well sealed. Repeat with the other 2 cooked eggs.

**continued overleaf**

Roll each coated egg around on the flour plate until lightly dusted on all sides. Next, coat well in the beaten egg, then roll around on the breadcrumb plate until tightly coated. Repeat to make 3 Scotch eggs.

Heat or preheat the air fryer to 190°C/375°F. Generously grease the base of the air fryer basket or crisping tray by spraying it with oil.

Place the Scotch eggs in the air fryer, making sure they aren't touching, then generously spray with oil. Air fry for 10–12 minutes, turning them halfway through and spraying generously with oil once more, or until the breadcrumbs are golden brown.

## TIP

Getting the perfect soft-boiled finish on your eggs can take a little practice, because all air fryers are likely to vary a little from model to model in how fast they heat up and maintain temperature etc. The timing and temperature given for air frying the eggs in this recipe assumes the air fryer is heating from being cold. If you preheat your air fryer first or your air fryer is already hot from cooking something else beforehand, then shave at least 2 minutes off the cooking time.

# 'ROASTED' VEGGIES

 Once cooked and cooled, freeze for up to 3 months. Air fry from frozen at 200°C/400°F for 7-10 minutes.

- 3 tbsp olive oil or garlic-infused oil, for drizzling
- ½ tsp salt

## Use any 3 veggies from below

- 1 medium red/green/yellow (bell) pepper, chopped into 2.5cm (1 inch) chunks
- 200g (7oz) cherry tomatoes
- 1 medium courgette (zucchini), chopped into 5mm (¼ inch) discs
- 1 small broccoli, cut into 4cm (1½ inch) florets
- 1 small red onion, peeled and quartered
- ½ cauliflower, cut into 4cm (1½ inch) florets
- 1 medium-sized sweet potato or Maris Piper potato, chopped into 2cm (¾ inch) cubes
- ½ medium butternut squash, peeled and cut into 2cm (¾ inch) cubes
- 1 small aubergine (eggplant), chopped into 2cm (¾ inch) cubes

**Serves 2-3 / Takes 25 minutes**

Though this recipe might not be the mind-blowing gluten-free reunion you've been dreaming about, it does aim to be infinitely useful when pondering what to serve alongside your other wondrous air fryer creations. I've now completely retired roasting veggies in the oven, not just because it's twice as fast to do it in the air fryer, but also just because veg like sweet potato, butternut squash, potato and aubergine (eggplant) come out so much crisper! Simply choose any three of the veg listed to the left and 'roast' away, or use my suggestions below for inspiration:

- **Traffic light veg:** 1 red (bell) pepper, 1 courgette (zucchini) and 1 sweet potato

- **'Throw into a stir fry' veg:** 1 green (bell) pepper, 1 broccoli and 1 small red onion

- **'Throw into a curry' veg:** 1 yellow (bell) pepper, 1 cauliflower, 1 sweet potato

- **Roasted sweet potato and butternut squash:** 1 medium sweet potato and 1 butternut squash

- **'Roasted' broccoli and cauliflower:** 2 broccoli and ½ cauliflower

- **Mediterranean veg:** ½ yellow (bell) pepper, ½ quantity cherry tomatoes, ½ courgette (zucchini), ½ small red onion and 1 aubergine (eggplant)

- **'Roasted' potatoes and onion:** 1 small red onion and 2 Maris Piper potatoes

**continued overleaf**

Place your chosen prepared veg in a large bowl, add the oil and salt, then mix until everything is well coated.

Heat or preheat the air fryer to 180°C/350°F. Add everything to the air fryer in a flat, even layer, ensuring it isn't too piled up (which would greatly prolong the cooking time). Cook in smaller batches to avoid this, or use both drawers if you have a two-drawer air fryer.

Air fry for 18–20 minutes, turning them over halfway through, until all the veggies are softened and slightly blackened at the edges or golden brown. If your veggies are mostly in a single layer, this timing should be absolutely perfect, but if they're a little more piled up, consider turning them over two or three times during cooking instead of just once.

## TIPS

The vegetables can have wildly different cooking times depending on how big/thick you chop them – that's why I've specified measurements to ensure they all cook for the same time within the temperature and timings given. I've also specified quantities based on how much will fit into your average air fryer without piling everything up excessively, as this can greatly prolong cooking time.

To check if the vegetables are done, poke the veg that ordinarily takes the longest to cook (cauliflower, sweet potato, Maris Piper potato, butternut squash, aubergine/eggplant) with a fork. If it goes in easily and is fork tender, then everything else will be done too because these are the vegetables that always take the longest.

# BLUE CHEESE LOADED POTATO SKINS

**DF** Use a dairy-free alternative to Cheddar/blue cheese that melts well. Use a dairy-free milk and sour cream.

**LL** Use lactose-free milk and lactose-free sour cream.

**F** Use lactose-free milk, garlic-infused oil instead of garlic paste, and serve with no more than 40g (1½oz) sour cream per person.

**V** Use 100g (3½oz) black beans (drained weight) instead of ham.

**VE** Combine dairy-free and veggie advice and use vegan mayo.

**❄** Once cooked and cooled, freeze the loaded potato skins for up to 3 months. Air fry from frozen at 180°C/350°F for 7-10 minutes until crisp and piping hot in the middle.

- 800g (1lb 12oz) small-medium Maris Piper potatoes
- Vegetable oil in a spray bottle, for greasing
- 65g (2¼oz) blue cheese, crumbled
- ¼ tsp each of salt and ground black pepper
- 5 tbsp milk
- 2 tbsp finely chopped chives, plus an extra 3 tbsp to serve
- 65g (2¼oz) Cheddar, grated
- 100g (3½oz) thick-cut ham, sliced into thin strips (or use my gammon on page 109)

**For the sour cream and chive dip**
- 140g (⅔ cup) sour cream
- 40g (3 tbsp) mayonnaise
- 1 tsp garlic paste or 1 tbsp garlic-infused olive oil
- 3 tsp lemon juice
- Pinch each of salt and ground black pepper
- 2 tbsp finely chopped chives

**Serves 4 / Takes 35 minutes + cooling time**

**A combo of the microwave and air fryer makes these dangerously simple to throw together. Stuffed with a blue cheese and chive mash, encased in a golden, crispy skin and topped with chunky ham and golden cheese, these are the perfect starter, side or party food canapé that everyone will remember.**

Place the potatoes on a dinner plate and loosely cover with another plate. Microwave for 10 minutes (900W) until you can easily pierce them with a skewer all the way through without much resistance. Allow to cool for 10–15 minutes.

Slice each potato in half lengthways. Use a tablespoon to scoop out the flesh of each potato as if you were creating a 'potato bowl', leaving around a 4mm (⅛ inch) layer of potato inside. Place the flesh into a medium bowl.

Heat or preheat the air fryer to 200°C/400°F. Lightly grease the base of the air fryer basket or crisping tray by spraying it with a little oil.

Place the potato shells skin-side up in the air fryer (don't pile them on top of each other) and generously spray with oil. Air fry for 9–10 minutes, flipping halfway through and generously spraying with oil once more.

Meanwhile, add the blue cheese, salt, pepper, milk and chives to the scooped out potato flesh, then mash until smooth.

Spoon the mashed potato back into the potato shells, flattening it down using the back of the spoon. Sprinkle the Cheddar on top of each, followed by the ham.

Air fry for 8 more minutes until the ham is slightly singed at the edges and the cheese has browned. Meanwhile, mix together the ingredients for the sour cream dip in a small bowl.

Serve the loaded potato skins with the sour cream dip, alongside my Parmesan chicken tenders (page 158), spicy bean burgers (page 96), chicken Kyivs (page 110).

# CRISPY ONION RINGS

 Once cooked and cooled, freeze for up to 3 months. Air fry from frozen at 200°C/400°F for 5-6 minutes until crisp.

- 1 large egg
- 2 tbsp gluten-free plain (all-purpose) flour or cornflour (cornstarch)
- Pinch each of celery salt and ground white pepper
- 100g (scant 1½ cups) gluten-free breadcrumbs (page 24)
- 2 medium onions, cut into 1cm (½ inch) slices and separated into rings
- Vegetable oil in a spray bottle, for greasing

Serves 4 / Takes 15 minutes

You must all absolutely promise me one thing: that you'll make and enjoy these as much as physically possible! I've been mega intolerant to onion for years so I wasn't even able to try these personally, but I absolutely had to include this recipe for anyone out there who can enjoy them without problems. So please enjoy these on my behalf – I'm told they taste absolutely out of this world!

Beat the egg in a small bowl with a fork. Spread the flour out on a large dinner plate and mix in the celery salt and white pepper, then spread the breadcrumbs out on another large dinner plate.

Take the onion rings and dredge in the flour until lightly dusted on all sides, then dip each into the beaten egg bowl until coated. Next, place in the breadcrumbs until tightly covered.

Heat or preheat the air fryer to 200°C/400°F. Generously grease the base of the air fryer basket or crisping tray by spraying it with oil.

Place the coated onion rings in the air fryer basket, spray generously with oil and air fry for 8–10 minutes until golden, turning them over halfway through.

Serve in or alongside my zinger burger (page 138), bean burger (page 96) or salmon burger (page 88), or as part of a party food platter alongside my cheeseburger spring rolls (page 166), chicken wings (page 59), Parmesan chicken tenders (page 158) and loaded potatoes (page 178).

# 3-INGREDIENT YORKSHIRE PUDDINGS

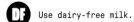 Use dairy-free milk.

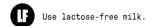 Use lactose-free milk.

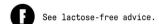 See lactose-free advice.

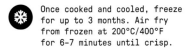 Once cooked and cooled, freeze for up to 3 months. Air fry from frozen at 200°C/400°F for 6-7 minutes until crisp.

- 2 tbsp vegetable oil
- 100g (¾ cup + 1 tbsp) cornflour (cornstarch)
- 3 medium eggs
- 150ml (⅝ cup) milk

**Makes 6 individual or 3 large / Takes 20 minutes**

**If you have mini pudding moulds (the kind you'd ordinarily make a small steamed sponge pudding in, for example) then you're already on your way to making some of the crispest, quickest Yorkshire puddings on Earth. You'll need quite a few of them – six ideally – so you don't have to make more than two batches, unless you don't mind making larger Yorkshire puds in foil containers/silicone air fryer liners – just remember not to overfill them!**

Heat or preheat the air fryer to 200°C/400°F.

Divide the oil between either six 8cm (3 inch) mini pudding moulds or three 15 x 20cm (6 x 8 inch) foil containers/silicone air fryer liners, place in the air fryer (or as many as will fit in your air fryer) and heat for at least 3 minutes (oil can burn and smoke so don't heat it for too much longer than this, although it should be scorching hot for best results!).

Add the cornflour and eggs to a large jug (pitcher) and whisk together until smooth. Add the milk gradually, whisking all the time until free of lumps, before pouring in the next addition.

Divide the batter equally between the 6 hot mini pudding moulds or 3 foil containers/silicone air fryer liners. Air fry for 12–15 minutes until risen, puffy and crisp. If you couldn't fit them all in at once, remove the Yorkshire puddings and keep them warm, then repeat the process with the remaining batter. Alternatively, you can save the batter for another day by keeping it covered in the fridge for up to 2 days (stir well before using).

Serve alongside your favourite roast dinner, such as my roast chicken (page 56) or toad in the hole (page 81), with roast potatoes (page 44), air-fried veggies (page 175) and lots of gluten-free gravy.

## TIP
Don't overfill the mini pudding moulds with oil, otherwise the batter will be too soggy to crisp up!

# QUICK BREADS

Whether you fancy a naan, flatbread or garlic bread baguette to serve alongside your main course, or slices of soda bread for submerging into soup or stews, that shouldn't mean you need to spend hours proving dough or gazing through your oven door as it bakes.

Yep, that's right – gluten-free bread can most definitely be quick when using these no-yeast, no-proving recipes that'll speed up the preparation process greatly, with the air fryer achieving the perfect bake in next to no time at all.

You'll find a variety of different approaches to breads-done-quick in this chapter, from my 'magic' yoghurt dough (no, it doesn't taste like yoghurt!) to tapioca starch dough, as well as recipe hacks to liven up store-bought gluten-free bread products. See page 25 for more info on tapioca starch and gluten-free white bread flour and where to find them.

# MOZZARELLA-STUFFED FLATBREAD

 V
Use a thick dairy-free yoghurt and dairy-free cheese.

 DF
Use lactose-free Greek yoghurt.

 LL
See low lactose advice.

 F
See dairy-free advice.

 VE

Once cooked and cooled, freeze for up to 3 months. Air fry from frozen at 200°C/400°F for 6-7 minutes until crisp.

- 200g (1½ cups) gluten-free self-raising flour, plus extra for dusting
- 100g (scant 1 cup) Greek yoghurt
- 70ml (scant ⅓ cup) water
- 50g (1¾oz) Red Leicester cheese, finely grated
- Small handful of grated mozzarella
- Vegetable oil in a spray bottle, for greasing

**Makes 4 / Takes 20 minutes**

**These cheese-stuffed flatbreads are the perfect accompaniment to tons of the recipes you'll find in this book, as well as dangerously quick to throw together. With a light, crisp exterior and fluffy middle that's packed with stringy, oozing cheese, fresh gluten-free bread has never tasted so good.**

In a large bowl, combine the flour, yoghurt (give it a good stir before using), water and Red Leicester cheese. Mix thoroughly using a spatula to ensure there are no hidden clumps of yoghurt-coated flour. As it starts to come together, use your hands to bring it into a slightly sticky ball.

Knead the dough briefly in the bowl until smooth, combined and no longer sticky. Dough still too sticky? Add a little more flour to the dough. Dough too dry? Add a little more water.

Transfer the dough to a medium sheet of lightly floured non-stick baking parchment. Divide the dough into 4 equal portions and roll each into a ball. Place three of the dough portions back in the bowl and cover.

Lightly flour the rolling pin and roll out one portion into a circle, about 2–4mm (⅛ inch) thick, ensuring it's symmetrical and not thicker or thinner in certain areas. Re-flour the rolling pin as necessary to stop it from sticking to the dough.

Scatter a thin layer of the grated mozzarella on the left side of the flatbread, leaving a 1cm (½ inch) clear space around the edges. Fold the opposite side over, using the baking parchment to support it, then peel back the baking parchment and press down at the edges to seal. Flatten down with your hands, then use the rolling pin to briefly roll it again until it's a flatbread shape about ½cm (¼ inch) thick. If the edges are a little jagged, feel free to neaten them up by running a small, sharp knife around the flatbread.

**continued overleaf**

Use a pair of sharp scissors to trim the paper around the flatbread, ensuring you leave no more than 1cm (½ inch) of excess paper. Repeat with the rest of the dough portions until you have 4 flatbreads, each on its own sheet of baking parchment, then very lightly spray each one all over with a little oil on top.

Heat or preheat the air fryer to 200°C/400°F.

Lift one flatbread into the air fryer (or as many as will comfortably fit at once) and air fry for 6–7 minutes, flipping it halfway through (discard the paper after flipping) and lightly spraying all over with oil once again. Repeat for the remaining flatbreads and serve as a side for mopping up sauce, scooping up dips, with my falafel and tahini sauce (page 114) or fold and fill for a quick and easy lunch.

## TIPS

For plain flatbreads, simply omit the Red Leicester cheese from the dough and skip the stage when you stuff the breads with mozzarella, then proceed with the rest of the recipe.

For any of the quick bread recipes that call for it (as well as the pizza on page 144) you can always use a thick natural yoghurt instead of Greek yoghurt as a like-for-like substitute.

# GARLIC AND CORIANDER NAAN 2.0

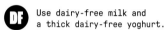
Use dairy-free milk and a thick dairy-free yoghurt.

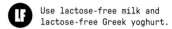
Use lactose-free milk and lactose-free Greek yoghurt.

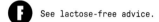
See lactose-free advice.

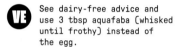
See dairy-free advice and use 3 tbsp aquafaba (whisked until frothy) instead of the egg.

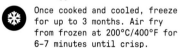
Once cooked and cooled, freeze for up to 3 months. Air fry from frozen at 200°C/400°F for 6-7 minutes until crisp.

- 225g (1¾ cups) gluten-free white bread flour, plus extra for dusting
- 90g (scant ½ cup) Greek yoghurt
- 60ml (4 tbsp) milk
- 1 large egg
- 1 tsp salt
- 1 tsp nigella seeds (optional)
- 4 tbsp garlic-infused oil
- Handful of coriander (cilantro), chopped, to serve

**Makes 4 / Takes 25 minutes**

Introducing a new and improved version of my 'real deal' garlic and coriander (cilantro) naan that featured in my second book, *How to Bake Anything Gluten Free*. However, I've not only adapted the method to be air fryer-friendly, I've made it even faster to whip these up and ensured that they now use entirely supermarket-stocked ingredients. They might even be lighter and more 'bready' in texture too!

The use of milk and egg makes the cooked naan super soft and pillowy, but crucially allows it to achieve more puff and bubbles when air fried. Of course, this also makes the dough a little wetter to work with, so flouring your hands and baking parchment is important to ensure it doesn't stick. If you have the time, allow the dough to rest for 10 minutes after it's been kneaded – this will allow the dough to hydrate and become a little less sticky as a result (that's optional though!).

In a large bowl, combine the flour, yoghurt (give it a good stir before using), milk, egg, salt and nigella seeds, if using. Mix thoroughly using a spatula to ensure there are no hidden clumps of yoghurt-coated flour. As it starts to come together, use your hands to bring it together into a slightly sticky ball.

Knead the dough briefly in the bowl until smooth and combined, but still a little sticky and loose.

Transfer the dough to a medium sheet of lightly floured non-stick baking parchment. Divide the dough into 4 equal portions and roll each into a ball. Place three of the dough portions back in the bowl, covered.

Using floured hands, gradually push one dough portion down into a naan shape, to about 2–4mm (⅛ inch) thick, ensuring it's not thicker or thinner in certain areas; keep lightly re-flouring your hands whenever it starts to stick to them.

**continued overleaf**

Use a pair of sharp scissors to trim the paper around the naan, ensuring you leave no more than 1cm (½ inch) of excess paper. Repeat with the rest of the dough portions until you have 4 naan, each on its own sheet of baking parchment, then very lightly brush each one all over with garlic-infused oil.

Heat or preheat the air fryer to 200°C/400°F.

Lift one naan into the air fryer (or as many as will comfortably fit at once) and air fry for 5 minutes, flipping it halfway through (discard the paper after flipping) and lightly brushing all over with garlic oil once again. After flipping, it should puff up and bubble. Repeat for any remaining naan that wouldn't fit into the air fryer.

Sprinkle with the chopped coriander and serve alongside your favourite curries.

## TIP

Gluten-free white bread flour can be found in the free from aisle or gluten-free section of supermarkets. Usually, I opt for using tapioca starch in conjunction with gluten-free self-raising flour for this recipe, as tapioca starch adds a bread-like, tear-able texture. However, the gluten-free white bread flour I use has tapioca starch in the blend already so it works perfectly here and eliminates the need for an extra ingredient! See page 25 for more info on gluten-free white bread flour (including which brand I used) and tapioca starch.

# GARLIC BREAD BAGUETTES

 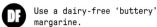

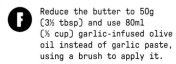 Use a dairy-free 'buttery' margarine.

Reduce the butter to 50g (3½ tbsp) and use 80ml (⅓ cup) garlic-infused olive oil instead of garlic paste, using a brush to apply it.

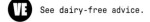 See dairy-free advice.

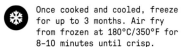 Once cooked and cooled, freeze for up to 3 months. Air fry from frozen at 180°C/350°F for 8-10 minutes until crisp.

- 2 store-bought gluten-free baguettes

**For the garlic butter**
- 150g (⅔ cup) butter, softened
- 3 tsp dried or finely chopped fresh parsley
- ½ tsp salt
- 3 tsp garlic paste

**Serves 4 / Takes 20 minutes**

**Garlic bread used to be a side that I never thought twice about. But after embarking on a gluten-free diet, it suddenly became something I could only dream about. With a crisp golden crust that's slathered in garlic butter, I guess my dreams finally came true! Awkwardly enough, I'm actually intolerant to garlic, so I use garlic-infused oil instead (see the FODMAP key notes for guidance on doing the same), but you can also use garlic paste for a stronger flavour, if you can tolerate it.**

In a small bowl, mix the ingredients for the garlic butter. If using garlic-infused oil (see above), ensure it's all well incorporated and smooth.

Cut both baguettes in half to make 4 short lengths, then cut deep slits every 2cm (¾ inch) without cutting through them completely. Smear the garlic butter over the tops, sides and down each slit of all 4 portions, then wrap each one separately in foil.

Heat or preheat the air fryer to 180°C/350°F.

Add all 4 wrapped baguette portions to the air fryer and air fry for 14–16 minutes, then peel back the foil to serve.

Enjoy alongside my chicken and bacon pasta bake (page 74), lasagne (page 90) or pesto and pea gnocchi (page 77).

# AIR FRYER SODA BREAD

 Use dairy-free milk.

 Use lactose-free milk.

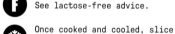 See lactose-free advice.

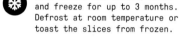 Once cooked and cooled, slice and freeze for up to 3 months. Defrost at room temperature or toast the slices from frozen.

- 330ml (1⅓ cups + 2 tsp) milk
- 5 tbsp lemon juice
- 300g (2¼ cups) gluten-free white bread flour
- ½ tsp xanthan gum
- ½ tsp salt
- 1 tsp bicarbonate of soda (baking soda)
- 2 tbsp olive oil

**Makes 1 loaf / Takes 35 minutes + resting**

**Who knew that you could turn six humble ingredients into freshly baked gluten-free soda bread? There's no yeast required for this recipe, so it's pretty quick as far as bread making goes. It has a soft crust and a lovely, light texture in the middle. If you're new to baking gluten-free bread, this is a great place to start.**

Add the milk and lemon juice to a jug (pitcher) and briefly mix. Allow to stand for 10–15 minutes until the mixture becomes thicker and a little lumpy.

Add the flour, xanthan gum, salt and bicarbonate of soda to a large bowl and mix until well combined. Once the milk mixture is ready, pour it in, followed by the oil. Mix well with a wooden spoon until smooth and it resembles a thick cake batter.

Scrunch up a medium sheet of non-stick baking parchment, then spread it flat again and use it to loosely line either a 15cm (6 inch) or 20cm (8 inch) round baking tin (pan) or pie dish. Use whichever cooking vessel will fit into your air fryer.

Scrape the mixture into the lined tin and smooth over the top so it's nice and flat. Trim the excess overhanging paper, cover with a tea (dish) towel and allow to rest at room temperature for no less than 30 minutes and no more than 1 hour.

Heat or preheat the air fryer to 200°C/400°F. You'll need to preheat your air fryer for this one, so if your air fryer doesn't force a short preheating period when you turn it on, simply set it to 200°C/400°F and wait 2 minutes.

Place the tin in the air fryer and air fry for 10 minutes, then reduce the temperature down to 170°C/340°F and air fry for a further 15 minutes. If making in a 15cm (6 inch) tin, flip the loaf over and air fry for a final 5 minutes.

Remove from the air fryer, carefully remove from the baking tin and tap the base to check that it feels and sounds hollow – if so, it's done; if not, simply air fry for a little longer. Place on a wire rack to cool completely before slicing.

# TORTILLA BOWLS

DF  LL  F  V  VE

❄ Once cooked and cooled, freeze for up to 3 months. Air fry from frozen at 200°C/400°F for 4-5 minutes until crisp.

- 2 store-bought gluten-free tortillas
- Vegetable oil in a spray bottle, for greasing
- Fillings of your choice

Serves 2 / Takes 10 minutes

Whenever the air fryer can effortlessly transform a store-bought gluten-free product into something fun and imaginative, you can bet I'm first in line to do so! Using two 12cm (5 inch) heatproof bowls, you can easily create edible tortilla bowls that are perfect for loading with fajita filling (page 134) or even chilli con carne. I simply use two Pyrex glass bowls, which I normally use for baking; mine are safe to use up to 300°C/570°F, so check your bowls first to ensure they are too!

Take one of the tortillas and lightly spray with oil on both sides, then push into the first heatproof bowl. Place the second heatproof bowl on top until it's snugly in place.

Heat or preheat the air fryer to 200°C/400°F. Place the two arranged bowls in the air fryer for 5–6 minutes, then carefully remove the outer bowl (the heatproof bowl inside the tortilla wrap should remain) and continue to air fry for 2–3 minutes. Repeat with the other tortilla.

Fill the tortilla bowl with steak or chicken fajita filling (page 134) and finish with your favourite toppings, such as smashed avocado, salsa, sour cream and grated cheese.

# ULTIMATE CHEESY DOUGH BALLS

V

DF
Use a hard dairy-free alternative to butter, dairy-free milk and cheese.

LL
Use lactose-free milk.

F
See low lactose advice.

❄
Once cooked and cooled, freeze for up to 3 months. Air fry from frozen at 200°C/400°F for 6-8 minutes until crisp.

- 175g (1⅓ cups) gluten-free white bread flour, plus extra for dusting
- 55g (⅓ cup) tapioca starch (page 25)
- ½ tsp xanthan gum
- 2½ tsp gluten-free baking powder
- 60g (2¼oz) extra-mature Cheddar, grated
- ½ tsp salt
- 1 large egg
- 150ml (⅝ cup) milk
- 35g (2½ tbsp) butter, melted
- 60g (2¼oz) mozzarella

Makes 16 / Takes 20 minutes + resting

**These might just be my best ever dough balls yet, which are even lighter and fluffier, yet still just as crisp and crusty outside, with an intense explosion of cheese in the middle.**

Add the flour, tapioca starch, xanthan gum, baking powder, grated Cheddar and salt to a large bowl. Mix until well combined, then add the egg, milk and melted butter and mix everything together until smooth and combined (I use an electric hand whisk for this part).

Cover and allow to rest for around 10 minutes, so the dough can hydrate.

Lightly flour your hands and work surface. Take about 30g (1oz) of the dough and flatten it down with your hands, then place a small piece of mozzarella in the centre. Bring the dough together and roll it up to enclose the cheese. Repeat with the rest of your mixture.

Place the dough balls on individual pieces of non-stick baking parchment.

Heat or preheat the air fryer to 180°C/350°F. Add the dough balls to the air fryer and fry for 6–8 minutes, until golden. Remove from the air fryer and allow to cool a little before enjoying warm.

Serve as a starter alongside hot pizza sauce as a dip, or with your favourite pasta dish, such as my chicken and bacon pasta bake (page 74), pesto and pea gnocchi (page 77) or lasagne (page 90).

# SANDWICH THINS

 Use a hard dairy-free alternative to butter.

 Use lactose-free milk.

 See low lactose advice.

 Once cooked and cooled, freeze for up to 3 months. Air fry from frozen at 200°C/400°F for 6-8 minutes until crisp.

- 175g (1⅓ cups) gluten-free white bread flour, plus extra for dusting
- 55g (⅓ cup) tapioca starch
- ½ tsp xanthan gum
- 2½ tsp gluten-free baking powder
- ½ tsp salt
- 1 large egg
- 125ml (½ cup + 1 tsp) milk
- 35g (2½ tbsp) butter, melted, plus extra (optional) to finish

**Makes 8 / Takes 20 minutes + resting**

**These days sandwich thins are my go-to when it comes to making my own lunch for when I'm on-the-go. Luckily for me, it couldn't be quicker or easier to whip up a batch, ready to cram with all my favourite fillings.**

Add the flour, tapioca starch, xanthan gum, baking powder and salt to a large bowl. Mix until well combined, then add the egg, milk and melted butter. Mix everything together until smooth and combined (I use an electric hand whisk for this part).

Cover and allow to rest for around 10 minutes, so the dough can hydrate.

Lightly flour your hands and work surface. Take a 55g (2oz) portion of the dough and flatten it down with your hands initially, followed by rolling it with a rolling pin to get it into a thin square sandwich size, about 10 x 10cm (4 x 4 inches). Prick with a fork a few times in the centre.

Place each sandwich thin on a square of baking parchment only slightly bigger than the dough.

Heat or preheat the air fryer to 180°C/350°F. Place as many as will comfortably fit into the air fryer and air fry for 8 minutes, until golden, flipping them and discarding the paper halfway through.

Remove from the air fryer and cover with a clean tea (dish) towel to help them soften up as they cool. Optionally brush each sandwich thin with a little melted butter while still hot to soften even further – I'd highly recommend you do, as it improves the texture of the finished product! Once fully cooled, carefully slice in half with a bread knife and fill with a sandwich filling of your choice.

# BAKERY-STYLE BREADSTICKS

 Use a smoked-dairy-free cheese instead of Parmesan.

 Use veggie-friendly Grana Padano instead of Parmesan.

 Once cooked and cooled, freeze for up to 3 months. Air fry from frozen at 200°C/400°F for 6-8 minutes until crisp.

- 175g (1⅓ cups) gluten-free white bread flour, plus extra for dusting
- 55g (⅓ cup) tapioca starch
- ½ tsp xanthan gum
- 2½ tsp gluten-free baking powder
- 1 tsp dried rosemary
- 45g (1½oz) Parmesan, grated, plus extra for sprinkling
- 40g (1½oz) pitted green olives, chopped
- ½ tsp salt
- 1 large egg
- 125ml (½ cup) water
- 35g (1¼oz) olive oil, plus extra for brushing
- Sesame seeds, for sprinkling

**Makes 10–12 / Takes 20 minutes + resting**

**Unlike the crunchy breadsticks you might be familiar with, these crusty, fluffy-in-the-middle ones are more akin to freshly baked bread, crammed with olives for the ultimate flavour punch. Not only is it hard to believe they don't contain yeast, nobody would ever guess in a million years that they're gluten-free! If you're not a big olive fan, you could use sun-dried tomatoes instead.**

Add the flour, tapioca starch, xanthan gum, baking powder, rosemary, Parmesan, olives and salt to a large bowl. Mix until well combined, then add the egg, water and olive oil. Mix everything together until smooth and combined (I use an electric hand whisk for this part).

Cover and allow to rest for around 10 minutes, so the dough can hydrate.

Lightly flour your hands and work surface. Take about 45g (1½oz) of the dough and roll it out between your palms into a breadstick about 12cm (4¾ inches) long, then repeat with the rest of your mixture.

Place the breadsticks on individual pieces of non-stick baking parchment (not much bigger than the breadsticks themselves), brush with a little olive oil and sprinkle some grated Parmesan and sesame seeds on top of each breadstick.

Heat or preheat the air fryer to 180°C/350°F. Place as many breadsticks as will comfortably fit in the air fryer and air fry for 10–12 minutes until there's a very slight change in colour – they will remain fairly pale.

Remove from the air fryer, allow to cool briefly, then enjoy warm or cold. Serve with my sweet potato and red pepper soup (page 72), salad, or on their own with a balsamic dip.

# THE SWEET STUFF

While most of us likely didn't buy air fryers to make sweet treats, that's probably because we weren't overly aware that it was even possible! But in reality, there's a whole wide world of classic bakes, proper desserts and deep-fried-turned-air-fried favourites that lie ahead.

And, of course, when you're gluten-free and your sweet options are usually either a brownie in plastic packaging, fruit salad or – even worse – absolutely nothing, that only makes the air fryer even more essential in the battle to reclaim everything you miss eating! Fortunately, the brownies you see me lovingly gazing at here were fresh from the air fryer (gooey, fudgy and addictive) and not from a plastic wrapper (which usually just taste like a chocolate sponge!).

I've endeavoured to include plenty of '3 ways' recipes here too, so you can get the most out of this chapter!

# AMERICAN PANCAKES

 V

 DF — Use dairy-free milk.

 LF — Use lactose-free milk.

 F — See lactose-free advice.

❄ Once cooked and cooled, freeze for up to 3 months. Air fry from frozen at 200°C/400°F for 5 minutes until crisp.

- 100g (¾ cup) gluten-free self-raising flour
- ½ tsp gluten-free baking powder
- 2 tbsp caster (superfine) sugar
- 100ml (generous ⅓ cup) milk
- 1 tsp vanilla extract
- 2 medium eggs
- Vegetable oil in a spray bottle, for greasing
- Maple syrup, to serve

 Makes 3 rectangular pancakes / Takes 15 minutes

**Fancy thick and fluffy pancakes without all the flipping? I tweaked the ratios of my usual pancake batter specifically for air frying, so don't expect results this good with any old gluten-free pancake recipe. For this one, I used foil containers that were smaller than the usual size mentioned elsewhere in this book – 15 x 11.5cm (6 x 4½ inch) – but if your containers are bigger than mine, just remember that you might need to give them an extra minute or two in the air fryer. You could also make these by simply greasing the base of your air fryer and pouring the pancake batter straight in (no foil container or air fryer liner required), but they'll be a little harder to remove once done!**

Mix the flour, baking powder and sugar in a large bowl. Add the milk and vanilla extract to a jug (pitcher) and crack in the eggs, then beat using a fork. Whisk one-third of the egg mixture into the dry ingredients at a time until you're left with a smooth batter the consistency of thick cream.

Heat or preheat the air fryer to 160°C/320°F. Lightly grease 3 foil containers or silicone air fryer liners with a few sprays of oil. Pour the pancake batter in until just under 1cm (½ inch) deep.

Place as many of the containers or liners in your air fryer as will comfortably fit and air fry for 6–8 minutes, or until you can poke the middle with a cocktail stick and it comes out clean. Repeat with any other containers or liners.

Allow to cool for 5 minutes, then carefully remove from the containers by flexing the container and turning out onto a plate. Serve with lots of maple syrup.

## TIP

Feel free to add a small handful of fresh blueberries, chocolate chips or sliced banana to the containers or air fryer liners immediately after pouring in the pancake batter.

# GRANOLA 3 WAYS

 **Chocolate hazelnut:** use dairy-free chocolate chips.

 **Chocolate hazelnut:** use lactose-free chocolate chips.

 Use maple syrup instead of honey. **Chocolate hazelnut:** use lactose-free chocolate chips.

**VE** Use maple syrup instead of honey. **Chocolate hazelnut:** use dairy-free chocolate chips.

- 75ml (5 tbsp) runny honey or maple syrup
- ½ tsp vanilla extract
- 25ml (1½ tbsp) vegetable oil or melted coconut oil
- 100g (1 cup) gluten-free oats
- 50g (1¾oz) gluten-free puffed rice cereal
- 20g (¾oz) desiccated (dried shredded) coconut
- Pinch of salt

**For pumpkin spice granola**
- 1 tsp ground cinnamon
- ½ tsp ground ginger
- ½ tsp ground nutmeg
- ½ tsp ground allspice
- 40g (1½oz) pumpkin seeds

**For honey nut granola (pictured)**
- 35g (1¼oz) pecans, chopped
- 20g (¾oz) flaked (slivered) almonds
- 1 tbsp ground almonds

**For chocolate hazelnut granola**
- 40g (1½oz) hazelnuts, chopped
- 50g (1¾oz) milk or dark chocolate chips

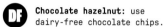

**Makes about 300g (10½oz) / Takes 20 minutes**

**Granola is one of those things that benefits hugely from the air fryer's unique way of intensely circulating hot air, while simultaneously expelling steam; the result is golden, extra-toasty, crunchy granola that an oven simply can't match. Perfect served with milk or creamy yoghurt.**

Add the honey or maple syrup, vanilla extract, vegetable/coconut oil, oats, rice cereal, desiccated coconut and salt to a large bowl, then mix together until everything is evenly coated, adding all the ground spices if making the pumpkin spice granola.

Heat or preheat the air fryer to 160°C/320°F (basket or crisping tray removed). Line the base with non-stick baking parchment (wait until it's preheated, if necessary).

Spoon the granola into the air fryer, trying not to pile it up, keeping everything in a single layer. Air fry for around 12–14 minutes, turning it over halfway through and adding in the nuts or seeds for your chosen variation. If you have a large air fryer it might take less time, a smaller air fryer may take a little longer – check on it a few minutes before it's done to ensure it's not darkening too much; it should be golden and toasted.

Remove the granola and spread out onto a baking tray to cool and to crisp up further. If making the chocolate hazelnut granola, mix in the chocolate chips once cooled.

Store the cooled granola in an airtight container for up to a month, and enjoy with milk or yoghurt.

# CHOCOLATE CHIP COOKIES 3 WAYS

**DF** Make only the **white chocolate and cranberry** or **triple chocolate** cookies using a hard dairy-free alternative to butter and dairy-free chocolate chips.

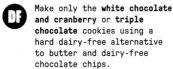 Make only the **white chocolate and cranberry** or **triple chocolate** cookies using lactose-free chocolate chips.

**F** See low lactose advice.

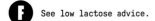 See dairy-free advice and replace the egg with 60ml (4 tbsp) dairy-free milk.

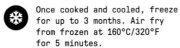 Once cooked and cooled, freeze for up to 3 months. Air fry from frozen at 160°C/320°F for 5 minutes.

- 125g (½ cup + 1 tbsp) butter, softened
- 100g (½ cup) light brown sugar
- 100g (½ cup) caster (superfine) sugar
- 1 tsp vanilla extract
- 1 large egg
- 300g (2¼ cups) gluten-free self-raising flour
- ¼ tsp xanthan gum
- ½ tsp bicarbonate of soda (baking soda)

**For white chocolate and cranberry**

- 125g (¾ cup) white chocolate chips
- 75g (2½oz) dried cranberries

**For triple chocolate**

- 25g (¼ cup) cocoa powder (reduce flour to 255g/2 cups)
- 100g (⅔ cup) milk chocolate chips
- 100g (⅔ cup) white chocolate chips

**For rainbow cookies**

- 200g (7oz) chocolate M&Ms (ensure gluten-free) or any other gluten-free sugar-coated chocolate treats

**Makes 30 / Takes 20 minutes + cooling**

**How do you enjoy freshly baked cookies without even turning the oven on? The answer: turn your air fryer into your own personal cookie factory!**

In a bowl, cream together the softened butter and both sugars until light and fluffy. Add the vanilla and egg, and mix in.

Add the flour (don't forget to reduce the amount if making triple chocolate cookies), xanthan gum and bicarb and mix in until a dough forms. Stir in the additions of your choice, then roll the dough into balls about 25–30g (1oz) each. Push a few more chocolate chips or M&Ms into the top, then flatten and round each ball like a hockey puck until about 1cm (½ inch) thick.

Place a cookie dough portion on a small square of non-stick baking parchment (trimmed to around 12cm/4¾ inches square) pierced with lots of holes (this is important to circulate the air and help them cook). Repeat with the rest of the portions.

Heat or preheat the air fryer to 160°C/320°F. Add as many cookies as will fit in the air fryer without the paper overlapping (I do 3 or 4 at a time) and air fry for 10–12 minutes until golden.

Once baked, leave to cool in the air fryer (closed) for 5 minutes, then use the baking parchment to lift them out and transfer to a wire rack to fully cool. Repeat with more of the cookie dough to make a full batch, or keep the dough in the fridge for up to 5 days, or the freezer, to air fry another day. (Defrost and/or bring the cookie dough up to room temperature before cooking, or you will find they cook faster on the outside than the inside.)

**TIP**

If the baking parchment isn't trimmed to be somewhere around the size given above, the excess paper can fly around and flap about in the air fryer, and if super over-sized it can even touch the heating element and burn. I'm sure you can guess how I came by this information!

# CHURROS

Makes 12–14 / Takes 30 minutes + cooling + chilling

V

DF
Use a hard dairy-free alternative to butter and serve with dairy-free caramel or chocolate sauce.

LL
Serve with lactose-free caramel or chocolate sauce.

F
See low lactose advice.

❄
Once cooked, cooled and coated, freeze for up to 3 months. Air fry from frozen at 200°C/400°F for 5 minutes until crisp.

- 250ml (1 cup + 2 tsp) water
- 75g (⅓ cup) butter
- 20g (1 tbsp + 1 tsp) caster (superfine) sugar
- 125g (1 cup minus 1 tbsp) gluten-free plain (all-purpose) flour
- ¼ tsp xanthan gum
- 1 tsp vanilla extract
- 3 medium eggs, beaten

**For the sugar coating**
- 2 tbsp butter, melted
- 4 tbsp caster (superfine) sugar

**To serve**
- Store-bought caramel sauce
- Store-bought chocolate sauce

**Though traditionally a deep-fried treat or requiring a dedicated churros maker, an air fryer can negate the need for either. Simply combine the churros mixture, pipe onto a baking tray and chill – then all that's left to do is air fry. With just a little spritz of oil, there's no doubt that these emerge healthier, though just as golden as you'd expect!**

In a pan, gently heat the water, butter and sugar until just boiling, then remove from the heat and quickly stir in the flour and xanthan gum really well until well combined and no lumps remain. Place the mixture into a large bowl and allow to cool for 10 minutes or so.

Add the vanilla and, a little at a time, the beaten eggs, mixing in between additions – I use an electric hand whisk for this part. You're looking for a smooth, thick and pipeable consistency. (You might not need all the egg, as eggs differ in size, so don't add it all if your mixture appears ready.)

Place the mixture in a piping (pastry) bag with a medium-large open star nozzle attached, then place a large sheet of non-stick baking parchment on a baking tray that'll comfortably fit into your fridge. Pipe short lines of the mixture onto the baking parchment and place in the fridge to chill for an hour. You might need a couple of trays, or you can leave the piping bag in the fridge to pipe more later.

Once chilled, cut the baking parchment tightly around each churro, so they are all on individual pieces.

Heat or preheat the air fryer to 180°C/350°F. Place as many churros as will comfortably fit in the air fryer and spray with a little oil to help with colouring. Air fry for 20 minutes until puffed and golden.

Remove from the air fryer and, while still warm, coat in the melted butter until lightly covered, followed by the sugar. Serve alongside your dips – I always have them warmed up!

## TIP

Once air fried, did you know that you can use the churros to make gluten-free chocolate éclairs? You do now! Once cooled, simply pipe sweetened whipped cream into the centres and top with melted chocolate.

# APPLE + CUSTARD HAND PIES OR CARAMEL APPLE TURNOVERS

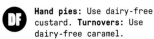

**Hand pies:** Use dairy-free custard. **Turnovers:** Use dairy-free caramel.

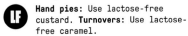

**Hand pies:** Use lactose-free custard. **Turnovers:** Use lactose-free caramel.

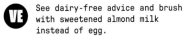

See dairy-free advice and brush with sweetened almond milk instead of egg.

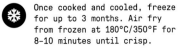

Once cooked and cooled, freeze for up to 3 months. Air fry from frozen at 180°C/350°F for 8-10 minutes until crisp.

- 280g (10oz) store-bought ready-rolled gluten-free puff pastry, about 24 x 30cm (9½ x 12 inches)
- 150g (5½oz) canned apple pie filling
- ¼ tsp ground cinnamon
- Store-bought custard (for the hand pies)
- Store-bought caramel sauce (for the turnovers)
- 1 egg, beaten
- 4 tbsp demerara sugar

**Makes 4 / Takes 25 minutes**

I think it's clear where the inspiration came from for these two apple-filled pastry treats: bakery-style apple turnovers and a certain fast food chain's apple pie, both of which are literally never gluten-free. Fortunately, the air fryer is great at achieving a golden, light and crispy finish on the pastry and ensuring that cinnamon-tinged apple filling is piping hot.

Remove the pastry from the fridge 10 minutes before starting – this makes it easier to unroll without breaking or cracking. In a small bowl, combine the apple pie filling and cinnamon.

Unroll the puff pastry on a flat work surface with a long side closest to you. Use a pizza cutter (I also use a long ruler to ensure I'm cutting straight) to cut horizontally, dividing the pastry into 2 equal strips.

**For apple + custard hand pies (pictured opposite):** Cut both strips vertically at 7.5cm (3 inch) intervals to create 8 rectangles.

Spoon a line of apple filling just off the centre of four of the rectangles. Spoon a line of thick custard alongside the apple.

On the paper the pastry was rolled up in, use a rolling pin to slightly roll and enlarge the remaining pastry rectangles (this will ensure they fit over the filling).

Brush the edges of the topped pastry rectangles with beaten egg, then place the other rectangles on top. Seal the edges using a fork and brush each with egg. Cut a couple of slits on top using a sharp knife and sprinkle with the demerara sugar.

**For caramel apple turnovers (pictured overleaf):** Cut both strips vertically at 12cm (4¾ inch) intervals to create 4 squares (use any excess to make a mini hand pie with any remaining filling).

Spoon a dollop of the apple filling into the centre of the squares and then drizzle with caramel sauce.

continued overleaf

Brush the edges of the squares with beaten egg, then take one corner of each and fold over diagonally so it meets the edge of the opposite corner to form a filled triangle. Seal the edges with a fork and brush with beaten egg. Cut a couple of slits on top using a sharp knife and sprinkle with demerara sugar.

**To cook:** Heat or preheat the air fryer to 180°C/350°F. Place as many pies/turnovers as will comfortably fit in the air fryer without touching and air fry for around 10 minutes or until puffed and golden. Serve hot or cold.

## TIP

The measurements given in the method are assuming that your puff pastry sheet is about 24 x 30cm (9½ x 12 inches). If your puff pastry sheet measurements are different, there's no need to panic! Instead of focusing on measurements, once you've divided your pastry sheet into two long strips, simply divide the strips into either 8 uniform rectangles (for hand pies) or 4 equal squares (for turnovers).

# DOUGHNUT HOLES OR MINI ICED BUNS

 **V**

 **DF** Use a hard dairy-free alternative to butter, and dairy-free milk.

 **LL** Use lactose-free milk.

 **F** See low lactose advice.

 Once cooked and cooled, freeze doughnut holes (ideally uncoated) and iced buns (must be without icing) for up to 3 months. Air fry from frozen at 200°C/400°F for 5 minutes until crisp. Allow iced buns to fully cool before following icing and decorating steps.

- 175g (1⅓ cups) gluten-free self-raising flour
- 55g (⅓ cup) tapioca starch
- ¼ tsp xanthan gum
- 60g (5 tbsp) caster (superfine) sugar
- 1 tsp gluten-free baking powder
- 1 large egg
- 150ml (⅝ cup) milk
- 35g (2 tbsp + 1 tsp) butter, melted and cooled

**For doughnut holes coating**
- 50g (3½ tbsp) melted butter, in a small bowl
- 50g (¼ cup) caster (superfine) sugar, in a small bowl
- Strawberry jam, for dipping

**For icing and decorating the mini iced buns**
- 125g (generous ¾ cup) icing (confectioners') sugar
- ½ tsp vanilla extract
- Colourful sprinkles (ensure gluten-free)

**Makes 12-14 buns or 24-28 holes / Takes 30 minutes**

**You can use this dough to make either cinnamon sugar doughnut holes or cute little bakery-style iced bun bites. Both are just as light and fluffy as each other, but with the finished coating/icing applied, you'd never know they started in the same bowl. Remember to check your local health food shop for tapioca starch or simply hop online to order a bag.**

Add the flour, tapioca starch, xanthan gum, sugar and baking powder to a large bowl and mix well. Add the egg, milk and melted butter and mix everything together until smooth and combined (I use an electric hand whisk for this part). Allow to rest and hydrate for about 10 minutes before placing in a piping (pastry) bag – no need for a piping nozzle.

Using non-stick baking parchment, cut out 5cm (2 inch) squares for the doughnut holes or 10 x 5cm (4 x 2 inch) rectangles for the iced buns. Snip off a 2cm (¾ inch) opening from the bottom of the piping bag. If making doughnut holes, pipe golf ball-sized balls onto each piece of the paper, and if making iced buns pipe a longer sausage shape.

Heat or preheat the air fryer to 180°C/350°F. Carefully place the piped dough in the air fryer, using the baking parchment to lift them and lower in. Don't put too many in at once so that the air can circulate well. Air fry for 6 minutes or until puffed and golden, then remove from the air fryer and discard the baking parchment.

**For the doughnuts:** dip straight into the melted butter until well coated, followed by the sugar, then serve with some jam to dip.

**For the iced buns:** allow the buns to cool for 15–20 minutes before decorating. In a small bowl mix together the icing sugar and vanilla extract and gradually add water 1 tablespoon at a time until you have a thick white glacé icing. Don't add too much water or it will become transparent and also run off the buns! Spoon over a layer on top of each bun and cover in sprinkles. Allow the icing to set for around 30 minutes.

# CHOCOLATE FONDANTS

**DF** Use a hard dairy-free alternative to butter, and dairy-free chocolate.

**LL** Use lactose-free chocolate.

**F** See low lactose advice.

❄ Freeze before cooking in freezer-friendly ramekins and either fully defrost and air fry using the temps/timings in the recipe, or air fry from frozen and add 3–4 minutes onto the cooking time.

- 100g (½ cup minus 1 tbsp) butter, plus extra for greasing
- 135g (4¾oz) dark chocolate
- 100g (½ cup) caster (superfine) sugar
- 2 large eggs
- 25g (3 tbsp) gluten-free plain (all-purpose) flour
- 10g (1½ tbsp) unsweetened cocoa powder

**Makes 4 / Takes 15 minutes**

**Never in a million years did I think that I'd be able to bake chocolate fondants with a gooey, molten chocolate middle in an air fryer... but here we are! This recipe is perfect for when your oven might still be busy cooking the main course; once the mixture is combined and in the ramekins, they can happily sit in a cold air fryer until everyone is ready for dessert. At that point simply air fry and serve.**

Butter 4 small ovenproof ramekins (mine are 10cm/4 inches in diameter) or 8cm (3 inch) mini pudding moulds.

In the microwave, melt together the butter and chocolate in a small bowl, mixing regularly in between short blasts. Allow to cool slightly. Alternatively, add the butter and chocolate to a large heatproof bowl set over a saucepan of gently boiling water, ensuring the water isn't touching the bowl. Stir until everything has melted and mixed together, then allow to cool slightly.

In a large bowl, whisk together the sugar and eggs until slightly frothy, then pour in the slightly cooled melted chocolate mixture and fold in. Fold in the flour and cocoa powder until combined.

Heat or preheat the air fryer to 180°C/350°F.

Pour or spoon the mixture into the prepared ramekins until around three-quarters full. Place in the air fryer basket and air fry for 8–10 minutes until risen. Carefully remove and invert each out onto a separate serving plate, then serve straight away for the perfect, gooey middle. Serve with a scoop of vanilla ice cream on top, if you like!

# MINI CRUMBLE 3 WAYS

 Use a hard dairy-free alternative to butter.

 Make only the pineapple crumble.

 See dairy-free advice

 Once cooked and cooled, portion into airtight containers and freeze for up to 3 months. Defrost in the fridge, then microwave at 900W until the middle is piping hot.

- 55g (¼ cup minus 1 tsp) cold butter
- 110g (¾ cup + 1½ tbsp) gluten-free plain (all-purpose) flour
- 45g (¼ cup) light brown sugar
- ½ tbsp ground cinnamon
- 25g (¼ cup) gluten-free oats (optional)

**For apple crumble**
- 600g (1lb 5oz) Bramley apples, peeled and chopped
- 1 tsp ground cinnamon
- 1 tbsp light brown sugar

**For pineapple crumble**
- 600g (1lb 5oz) fresh pineapple, peeled and chopped
- 1 tsp ground cinnamon (optional)

**For summer berry crumble (pictured)**
- 400g (14oz) frozen summer berries

**Makes 4 / Takes 25 minutes**

**There's no denying that the air fryer can't be beaten when it comes to getting that crispy, golden finish on your crumble, so why not celebrate that by making one of these three variations?**

For the crumble, rub the cold butter into the flour in a large bowl using your fingertips, until it resembles breadcrumbs. Or pulse together in a food processor for ease and speed.

Mix in the brown sugar, cinnamon and oats, if using, and put to one side.

Place your chosen fruit, along with any specified sugar and cinnamon, in an air fryer-safe dish that'll comfortably fit into your air fryer, add 2 tablespoons of water, mix and cover tightly with foil. (Make sure the foil is secure so that it doesn't become loose and get stuck in the air fryer's heating element!)

Heat or preheat the air fryer to 180°C/350°F. Air fry the fruit for 10 minutes until softened, mixing halfway through.

Place the fruit in the base of four 10cm (4 inch) ramekins until three-quarters full, then top each with the crumble mixture. Press it down a little and air fry for 10–12 minutes until the top is a little more golden and the fruit beneath is cooked.

Serve with custard or ice cream.

# COFFEE SHOP CUPCAKES

Use a hard dairy-free alternative to butter. **Cappuccino:** use dairy-free dark chocolate. **Caramel latte:** drizzle with dairy-free caramel.

**Cappuccino:** use lactose-free dark chocolate. **Caramel latte:** use lactose-free caramel.

See low lactose advice.

Once cooked, cooled and iced, freeze on a tray for 1–2 hours. When the buttercream is solid, transfer to airtight containers and freeze for up to 3 months. Defrost at room temperature.

- 170g (¾ cup) butter, softened
- 170g (¾ cup + 1½ tbsp) light brown sugar
- 170g (1¼ cups) gluten-free self-raising flour
- 3 eggs
- 1½ tbsp instant coffee mixed with 1½ tbsp boiling water
- ½ tsp gluten-free baking powder
- ¼ tsp xanthan gum

**For the buttercream**
- 150g (⅔ cup) butter, softened
- 300g (generous 2 cups) icing (confectioners') sugar

**For cappuccino cupcakes**
- 1 tsp vanilla extract
- 50g (1¾oz) dark chocolate, grated

**For caramel latte cupcakes**
- 1 tsp vanilla extract
- 100ml (⅓ cup) caramel sauce

**For Americano cupcakes**
- 1 tsp instant coffee mixed with 1 tsp boiling water
- 10–36 coffee beans

Makes 10–12 / Takes 30 minutes + cooling

**Though I'm still not a big coffee drinker myself, my love for coffee cake remains unwaveringly strong! So these cupcakes are dedicated to coffee lovers or just coffee-cake aficionados like me, with three options on the menu to choose from. Optionally get someone to shout your first name at maximum volume while simultaneously banging a coffee machine portafilter for that authentic coffee shop experience.**

In a large bowl, cream together the butter and sugar until light and fluffy (I use an electric hand whisk or a stand mixer for this part). Add the flour, eggs, coffee, baking powder and xanthan gum and mix until well combined. Spoon the mixture evenly into paper cupcake cases that line a suitably sized cupcake tin that fits into your air fryer. In the absence of a small cupcake tin that fits, simply place the filled paper cupcake cases into silicone cupcake cases instead. They'll perfectly support the paper case while being handled and air fried.

Heat or preheat the air fryer to 160°C/320°F. Place as many as will fit in the air fryer for 12–15 minutes until risen and cooked through. Check that they're cooked by sticking a skewer into the centre of a cupcake – if it comes out clean, they're done. Remove from the air fryer and allow to cool on a wire rack.

Meanwhile, make the buttercream. Mix the butter in a stand mixer on a medium speed or in a large bowl with an electric hand mixer for about 5 minutes or until pale. Add your icing sugar in 2 stages, beating for about 3 minutes between each addition. Add the vanilla extract or coffee mixture (depending on which variation you're making) and mix once more – it should be a perfect pipeable consistency.

Spoon your buttercream into a piping (pastry) bag with a large star or round nozzle attached, then pipe the buttercream on top of the cakes. If you don't want to pipe it, simply spoon it on top. If making all three flavour variations, I like to ice each different flavour in a different way (like in the photo opposite!). Finish with either grated chocolate, a drizzle of caramel sauce or some coffee beans, depending on the flavour you've made.

# FUDGIEST CHOCOLATE CHIP BROWNIES

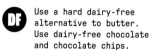 Use a hard dairy-free alternative to butter. Use dairy-free chocolate and chocolate chips.

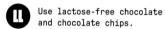 Use lactose-free chocolate and chocolate chips.

 See low lactose advice.

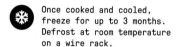 Once cooked and cooled, freeze for up to 3 months. Defrost at room temperature on a wire rack.

- 100g (½ cup minus 1 tbsp) butter
- 100g (3½oz) dark chocolate
- 2 large eggs
- 140g (¾ cup minus 2 tsp) caster (superfine) sugar
- 60g (½ cup minus 1 tbsp) gluten-free plain (all-purpose) flour
- 30g (4 tbsp) unsweetened cocoa powder, sifted
- ¼ tsp xanthan gum
- 60g (2¼oz) milk chocolate chips

**Makes 9 or 16 / Takes 35 minutes + chilling**

**Why make a brownie in the air fryer? Well, the short answer here is because you can! But as legend has it that air fryers make the fudgiest brownies known to mankind, I absolutely had to put that to the test. And it turns out that, thanks to the air fryer's intense circulation of hot air, it can bake the outside to perfection while applying delicate levels of heat to the middle, creating a brownie so fudgy that I highly recommend you chill them in the fridge before slicing to firm them up! The result is a fudgy brownie like no other, so make sure you give this recipe a try and judge for yourself.**

Add the butter and chocolate to a large heatproof bowl and place over a saucepan of gently boiling water, making sure the water isn't touching the bowl, and stirring until everything has melted and mixed together. Allow to cool to near room temperature. (You can also melt your butter and chocolate in the microwave in short bursts, stirring in between.)

In a large bowl, whisk the eggs and sugar until lighter in colour (I use an electric hand whisk or a stand mixer for this part). Pour the cooled, melted chocolate mixture into the egg and sugar mixture and carefully fold it in with a spatula until glossy and chocolatey in colour. Fold in the flour, cocoa powder and xanthan gum until well combined, then fold in the chocolate chips so that they are evenly distributed.

Heat or preheat the air fryer to 150°C/300°F

Pour the mixture into a container that fits into your air fryer (I've tried a 15cm/6 inch round baking tin/pan and an 18 x 11.5cm/7 x 4½ inch silicone liner) and air fry for around 25 minutes until the top is firm and it's no longer wobbling when gently shaken. Remove from the air fryer, allow to cool fully and then pop in the fridge for 2–3 hours to firm up and become super-fudgy.

Slice into 9 or 16 squares and enjoy cold or warmed up.

# BAKED BLUEBERRY AND LEMON CHEESECAKES

Once cooked and cooled, slice, wrap and freeze for up to 1 month. Defrost in the fridge.

- 80g (2¾oz) gluten-free digestive biscuits (Graham crackers)
- 35g (2 tbsp + 1 tsp) butter, melted
- 300g (1⅓ cups) full-fat cream cheese
- 15g (1¾ tbsp) gluten-free plain (all-purpose) flour
- 90g (½ cup minus 2½ tsp) caster (superfine) sugar
- 1½ large eggs, beaten
- 1 tsp vanilla extract
- Grated zest of 2 lemons and juice of ½ lemon
- 90g (scant 1 cup) sour cream
- 125g (4½oz) fresh blueberries

**For the blueberry topping**
- 125g (4½oz) fresh blueberries
- 1 tbsp lemon juice
- 50g (¼ cup) caster (superfine) sugar
- 1 tsp cornflour (cornstarch) mixed with 1½ tbsp water

**Makes 2 / Takes 40 minutes + cooling + chilling**

**Here's another show-stopping dessert that nobody would ever guess came out of the air fryer. I have two special tins for making these – small 10cm (4 inch) springform tins (pans) which are specifically designed for making individual mini cheesecakes. I bought mine in the kitchen section of a department store, but you can also buy them online.**

Firstly, make the base. In a food processor, blitz the biscuits to a crumb-like texture – not into a fine dust! Alternatively, pop them in a zip-lock bag and bash them with a rolling pin. Add to a large bowl and pour in the melted butter. Mix well.

Spoon the mixture into two 10cm (4 inch) loose-bottomed or springform tins (pans). Compact it into the base in an even layer, then chill in the fridge for around 30 minutes while you make the filling.

I use a electric hand whisk for this next part, but a stand mixer will do the job just fine too. If making by hand, ensure you mix for longer, until everything is well combined and consistent. Place the cream cheese in a large mixing bowl or the bowl of a stand mixer and mix on a low speed for 1 minute.

While mixing, gradually add the flour and sugar, maintaining the low speed. Next, gradually add the beaten egg along with the vanilla, lemon zest and juice.

Fold in the sour cream by hand, followed by the blueberries. Next, evenly spread the cheesecake filling on top of the chilled biscuit bases.

Heat or preheat the air fryer to 150°C/300°F. Place both cheesecakes in the air fryer and air fry for 30 minutes or until risen and golden on top. A skewer should come out clean when you poke it into the centre. Leave the cheesecakes in the air fryer, closed and switched off, for a further 30 minutes. After that, leave the air fryer drawer ajar to allow the cheesecakes to cool down.

Once cooled, cover the tins in foil (around the edges and underneath too), then place in the fridge to chill for around 4 hours.

Remove from the tins and transfer to serving plates.

**continued overleaf**

For the blueberry topping, place 50g (1¾oz) of the blueberries in a small pan with the lemon juice and sugar. Bring to a simmer over a medium heat, then allow the blueberries to break down. Mix in the cornflour slurry, which should make the mixture thicken, then stir through the rest of the blueberries and allow to cool. Add a small splash of water to thin it out if you feel it's too thickened once cooled.

Top the cheesecakes with the blueberries and either serve straight away or, ideally, chill briefly once more before serving.

### TIP

Not sure how to measure out half an egg? Place a bowl on some weighing scales and set it to zero, then crack an egg into it – you'll get the weight of a whole egg. Beat the egg so the yolk and white are combined and then pour half into a separate dish until the weight on the scales has halved. The other half can be kept for egg wash for use in other recipes, or simply use it when making scrambled eggs!

# CHERRY BAKEWELL SCONES

**V**

**DF** Use a hard dairy-free alternative to butter, and dairy-free milk.

**LL** Use lactose-free milk.

**F** Use lactose-free milk and omit the glacé cherries.

**VE** Use a hard dairy-free alternative to butter, and dairy-free milk. Brush with sweetened almond milk instead of egg.

❄ Once cooked and cooled, freeze for up to 3 months. Defrost at room temperature on a wire rack.

- 340g (2½ cups) gluten-free self-raising flour, plus extra for dusting
- 1 tsp gluten-free baking powder
- ¼ tsp xanthan gum
- 85g (⅓ cup + 2 tsp) cold butter, cubed
- 4 tbsp caster (superfine) sugar
- 75g (2½oz) glacé cherries
- 175ml (¾ cup) milk
- 3 tsp lemon juice
- 1½ tsp almond extract
- 1 egg, beaten

**Makes 7–8 / Takes 25 minutes**

**Though my classic gluten-free scones have kept me more than overjoyed for many years (especially as you literally can't tell the difference between them and gluten-containing scones), it's hard to believe it's taken me this long to remix them a little! So here it is: a tribute to another old favourite – cherry scones – but with an added Bakewell twist. And once again, the air fryer proves that it can take yet another classic bake in its stride!**

Add the flour, baking powder and xanthan gum to a large mixing bowl. Add the cold, cubed butter and rub it in with your fingers until you achieve a breadcrumb-like consistency, then stir in the sugar and glacé cherries.

Gently warm the milk in a jug (pitcher). I do this in the microwave at full power for about 35 seconds, but ensure that it doesn't get hot and remains lukewarm. Add the lemon juice to the warm milk and allow to stand for 1–2 minutes – it should look slightly curdled and lumpy when it's done. Next, add the almond extract to the milk mixture and beat together until well combined.

Make a well in the middle of the dry ingredients and pour in the milk mixture, working it in using a metal fork or knife. Keep working it till it forms a slightly sticky dough.

Lightly flour your hands and work surface. Remove the dough from the bowl and fold it over a few times to bring the dough together. Then bring the dough into a rounded shape about 3.5–4.5cm (1½–1¾ inches) thick. The taller, the better!

Using a 5cm (2 inch) round plain or fluted cookie cutter, push down into the dough and bring out your scones with the cutter. Gently push them out of the cutter and put to one side until you have used up all the dough. Instead of re-rolling the dough, keep re-rounding the dough back into a ball and continue to cut out your scones.

**continued overleaf**

Brush the tops of the scones with the beaten egg, then transfer onto individual pieces of non-stick baking parchment, ensuring each piece is only a little bigger than the base of each scone.

Heat or preheat the air fryer to 180°C/350°F. Pop the scones into the air fryer for about 10 minutes until golden on top.

Allow to cool briefly before enjoying warm, or allow to cool completely, then serve with jam and cream. Once cooled, store in an airtight container for 1–2 days or freeze for up to 3 months.

## TIP

Any of the scone recipes from my previous books (from fruit scones to cheese scones) can all be cooked in the air fryer using these timings.

# ECCLES CAKES

**DF** Use a dairy-free 'buttery' margarine.

**VE** See dairy-free advice and brush with sweetened almond milk instead of egg.

Once cooked and cooled, freeze for up to 3 months. Air fry from frozen at 180°C/350°F for 4-5 minutes until crisp.

- 280g (10oz) store-bought ready-rolled gluten-free puff pastry
- 10g (¼oz) dried mixed peel
- 20g (1 tbsp + 2 tsp) light brown sugar
- 5g (1 tsp) butter, softened
- ¼ tsp ground cinnamon
- 30g (1oz) currants
- Pinch of ground nutmeg
- 1 egg, beaten
- 5 tbsp caster (superfine) sugar

**Makes 6 / Takes 20 minutes**

**This traditional English bake, whose alternative names rather unappetizingly include 'squashed fly cake' and 'fly pie' (due to the look of the currants hiding inside the pastry), is a classic bake I've been craving for well over a decade. Fortunately, they're incredibly easy to make using store-bought gluten-free puff pastry and I'm pretty sure nobody would ever notice the difference. Oh and there are no squashed flies required either!**

Remove the pastry from the fridge 10 minutes before starting – this makes it easier to unroll without breaking or cracking.

In a small bowl, mix together the mixed peel, light brown sugar, butter, cinnamon, currants and nutmeg to form the filling.

Unroll the puff pastry on a flat work surface and roll the sheet a little using a rolling pin to make it slightly thinner all over. Use a 7.5cm (3 inch) cookie cutter to cut out 12 circles, then discard the excess.

Spoon around 1 teaspoon of the filling into the centre of six of the circles and brush beaten egg around the edge.

Roll the other half of the circles to be very slightly larger and press them down on top of the filling, securing around the edges by pressing down with your fingers. Carefully push down and flatten the pastry using your palm so you can almost see the filling through the top of the pastry.

Brush each with beaten egg, sprinkle with the caster sugar and use a sharp knife to make 3 slits down the centre of each.

Heat or preheat the air fryer to 180°C/350°F. Place as many in the air fryer as will comfortably fit without touching, then air fry for 8–10 minutes until golden.

Remove from the air fryer and enjoy warm or cold.

# VICTORIA SPONGE

**DF** Use a hard dairy-free alternative to butter.

❄ Once cooked, cooled and iced, slice then wrap individual slices and freeze for up to 3 months. Defrost unwrapped on a wire rack at room temperature.

- 170g (¾ cup) butter, softened, plus extra for greasing
- 170g (¾ cup + 1½ tbsp) caster (superfine) sugar
- 3 large eggs
- 1 tsp vanilla extract
- 170g (1¼ cups) gluten-free self-raising flour
- ½ tsp gluten-free baking powder
- ¼ tsp xanthan gum
- Strawberry or raspberry jam

**For the buttercream**
- 150g (⅔ cup) butter, softened
- 300g (generous 2 cups) icing (confectioners') sugar, plus extra for dusting
- 1 tsp vanilla extract

Serves 8 / Takes 40 minutes + cooling

I'm not sure how the judges would feel if you went on *The Great British Bake Off*, whipped your air fryer out and started baking a cake in it, but perhaps if they tried it, they'd soon see why you lugged it all the way into the tent! Though you'll need a smaller baking tin for this recipe than usual (my air fryer drawer won't fit anything bigger than a 15cm/6 inch baking tin/pan), that is the only change to my classic gluten-free Victoria sponge recipe. You can expect the same light and fluffy sponge, creamy vanilla buttercream and all the finishing touches to earn you star baker.

Lightly grease the bases of two 15cm (6 inch) round baking tins (pans) and line the base with non-stick baking parchment.

Add the butter, sugar, eggs, vanilla, flour, baking powder and xanthan gum to a large bowl. Mix for about 1 minute until well combined (I use an electric hand whisk or a stand mixer here).

Split the mixture evenly between the prepared tins.

Heat or preheat the air fryer to 150°C/300°F. Air fry the cakes for 25 minutes until golden on top and cooked through – check by sticking a skewer into the centre of one of the sponges: if it comes out clean, then it's done. The sponges may rise a little more in the centre than the outside. Allow to cool briefly in the tins then carefully invert onto a wire rack to fully cool.

While the sponges are cooling, make the buttercream. Mix the butter in a stand mixer on a medium speed or a large bowl using an electric hand mixer for about 5 minutes or until pale. Add your icing sugar in 2 stages, beating for about 3 minutes between each addition. Add the vanilla extract and mix once more; it should be a lovely smooth consistency.

To decorate, spread buttercream on one of your sponges, jam on the other and sandwich them together. Dust the top with a little extra icing sugar.

# CLOTTED CREAM SHORTBREAD

Once cooked and cooled, freeze for up to 3 months. Defrost at room temperature on a wire rack.

- 100g (½ cup minus 1 tbsp) butter, softened
- 100g (½ cup minus 1 tbsp) clotted cream
- 100g (½ cup) caster (superfine) sugar, plus a little (optional) to sprinkle
- 1 tsp vanilla extract
- 300g (2¼ cups) gluten-free plain (all-purpose) flour, plus extra for dusting
- ¼ tsp xanthan gum

**Makes 16 / Takes 20 minutes + chilling**

**Unlike regular shortbread, my clotted cream variation is a little lighter, crisper on the outside yet still with that signature melt-in-the-mouth texture. Perfect with anything from a cup of tea to a full-blown afternoon tea spread!**

In a large bowl, cream together the butter, clotted cream, sugar and vanilla extract using an electric hand whisk until light and fluffy (you can do this by hand; it will just take longer!).

Once combined, add in the flour and xanthan gum. Mix together once more, then use your hands to bring the dough together into a ball.

Wrap up the dough in cling film (plastic wrap) and allow it to sit in the fridge for at least an hour to firm up.

Once chilled, lightly flour a large sheet of non-stick baking parchment and roll out the dough to between 1cm and 1.5cm (½–⅔ inch) thick. Use a 6.5cm (2½ inch) fluted cookie cutter to cut out as many circles as possible, re-rolling and re-flouring the dough as necessary.

Place the biscuits on individual pieces of baking parchment, cut not much bigger than the biscuits themselves.

Heat or preheat the air fryer to 160°C/320°F. Place as many shortbread circles in the air fryer as will comfortably fit, using the baking parchment to lift them and lower in. Air fry for 12 minutes until slightly browning at the edges.

Allow to cool briefly in the air fryer before transferring to a wire rack to finish cooling. Repeat with any additional dough for further batches.

Optionally dust with a sprinkling of caster sugar to finish.

# STICKY BANOFFEE SELF-SAUCING PUDDINGS

Use a hard dairy-free alternative to butter and a dairy-free alternative to the cream.

Use lactose-free cream.

- 75g (2½oz) dates, pitted and chopped
- 75ml (5 tbsp) boiling water
- 50g (3½ tbsp) butter, softened, plus extra for greasing
- 50g (¼ cup) light brown sugar
- 1½ large ripe bananas, peeled and mashed
- 1 large egg
- 1 tsp vanilla extract
- 125g (1 cup minus 1 tbsp) gluten-free self-raising flour
- ¼ tsp xanthan gum

**For the sauce**
- 100g (½ cup) light brown sugar
- 100ml (generous ⅓ cup) double (heavy) cream
- 100ml (generous ⅓ cup) water

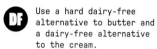

Makes 4 / Takes 20 minutes + soaking

**These all-in-one-desserts are the ultimate tribute to the combination of banana and toffee, with a soft, fluffy, steamed pudding-like sponge, and a sticky sauce hiding beneath. Simply serve with ice cream and thank your air fryer later! The mini dishes I use are 9 x 13cm (3½ x 5 inches) – see page 23 for more info.**

Soak the dates in the boiling water for about 30 minutes, then blitz using a stick blender to form a paste.

Butter 4 mini rectangular dishes that comfortably fit into your air fryer (see recipe intro).

In a large bowl, beat together the butter and sugar until light and fluffy. Add in the mashed banana, egg and vanilla extract. Mix together until well combined, then fold through the flour, xanthan gum and date paste.

For the sauce, heat the sugar, cream and water in a small saucepan over a medium heat, until just boiling and the sugar has dissolved.

Spoon the sponge mixture into the prepared dishes and carefully pour the sauce on top - it sounds weird, but trust me!

Heat or preheat the air fryer to 180°C/350°F. Place as many dishes into the air fryer as will comfortably fit and air fry for 12–15 minutes until golden and the top is cooked; a little of the sauce might be bubbling through. Leave to briefly cool for a few minutes before serving up with ice cream.

**TIP**

Make sure you don't overcook these puddings, or your sauce will disappear!

# 5-INGREDIENT CHOCOLATE HAZELNUT TWISTS

 V

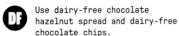 **DF** Use dairy-free chocolate hazelnut spread and dairy-free chocolate chips.

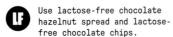 **LF** Use lactose-free chocolate hazelnut spread and lactose-free chocolate chips.

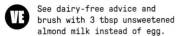 **VE** See dairy-free advice and brush with 3 tbsp unsweetened almond milk instead of egg.

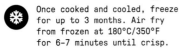 ❄ Once cooked and cooled, freeze for up to 3 months. Air fry from frozen at 180°C/350°F for 6-7 minutes until crisp.

- 280g (10oz) store-bought ready-rolled gluten-free puff pastry
- Chocolate hazelnut spread
- 100g (3½oz) milk chocolate chips
- 1 egg, beaten
- Icing (confectioners') sugar, for dusting

**Think crispy, light and puffy pastry twists with a gooey, oozing chocolate hazelnut filling. Store-bought gluten-free puff pastry makes this recipe an absolute doddle to make in no time, and the air fryer does the rest.**

Remove the pastry from the fridge 10 minutes before starting – this makes it easier to unroll without breaking or cracking.

Cut the sheet of pastry in half horizontally and spread one half with chocolate hazelnut spread, then sprinkle with the chocolate chips before sandwiching the other half of pastry on top.

Cut the pastry in 2cm (¾ inch) lengths and carefully twist each one twice. Place each chocolate twist on an individual piece of non-stick baking parchment (not much bigger than the twist itself) and brush each with beaten egg.

Heat or preheat the air fryer to 180°C/350°F. Place as many twists as will comfortably fit into the air fryer and air fry for about 10 minutes until golden.

Allow to cool a little and dust with icing sugar to finish.

# INDEX

# ABOUT THE AUTHOR

**Becky Excell** is a best-selling author and gluten-free food writer with a following of over 1 million on her social media channels and over 1 million monthly views on her award-winning blog, which recently celebrated its 10th birthday.

She won the *Observer Food Monthly*'s Best Food Personality award in 2022, the Blogosphere Award's Food Creator of the Year 2022 and BBC Food and Farming's Digital Creator of the Year Award 2023.

She's been eating gluten-free for 15 years and writes recipes for numerous print and online publications. She has made various TV appearances, most recently on ITV's *This Morning*, raising awareness and showing the nation how easy it is to make delicious gluten-free food, as well as cooking and baking at events including the BBC Good Food Show and The Big Feastival.

She gave up a career working in PR and marketing to focus on food full-time, with an aim to develop recipes which reunite her and her followers with the foods they can no longer eat. Her first five best-selling cookbooks, ***How to Make Anything Gluten Free***, ***How to Bake Anything Gluten Free***, ***How to Plan Anything Gluten Free***, ***Quick and Easy Gluten Free*** and ***Gluten Free Christmas*** were published by Quadrille. She lives in Essex, UK.

You can find more of Becky's delicious and fuss-free gluten-free recipes on her website **glutenfreecuppatea.co.uk**, on Instagram **@beckyexcell**, or on her Facebook page **Becky Excell Gluten Free**.

# THANK YOU

First of all, thank you to the 'Quad Squad' at Quadrille Publishing for all the clever publishing know-how and wizardry from start to finish. It allows us cooks to focus on what's most important to us – the recipes!

I'd like to personally thank Sarah Lavelle for her continued belief in not just me and my books, but in my entire gluten-free crusade as a whole. Thank you to super-star editor Harriet Webster for not just all the editing genius as always, but also for being so very present in the creation of this book – that's not something I thought was possible now you live in Austria! Thanks a million to editor Stacey Cleworth for jumping aboard too – I'm so happy to be able to work together.

Big thanks to my literary agent, Emily Sweet, who is always full of sage wisdom and guidance when I often feel very lost and drowning in a sea of emails that I don't have the answers for.

Thank you once again to my copy editor, Sally Somers, for your knowledgeable and insightful edits – the likes of which I now try to include in my drafts from the very beginning (I hope you can tell!).

A big high-five to designer, Emily Lapworth, for taking a basic mood board and turning it into a full-blown concept that radiates awesomeness from every page (as usual). And to Nikki Ellis for helping to get everything onto the page in a very small time frame!

Thank you to Hannah Hughes for all the truly mind-blowing food photography, open-mindedness and perhaps most importantly, a stellar photoshoot playlist. Shout out to photography assistant Sasha Burdian too, of course.

Thank you to Amy Stephenson for your flawless food-styling yet again (and baby Annie!), as well as food stylist assistants Valeria Russo and Sophie Pryn.

Huge thanks to prop stylist Max Robinson for the careful curation of props and construction of beautiful scenes, giving each recipe its own perfect stage and spotlight.

Thank you to Cat Parnell for her hair and make-up magic on set once again, which always helps me to feel more confident on camera! Thanks to Nicky for once again going out of her way to cut and colour my hair, and thank you to Amy for your amazing nail art skills.

Thanks to 'Team Laura' (Laura Willis and Laura Eldridge), Ruth Tewkesbury, Alice Hill as well as Iman Khabl and Diana Kojik for flying the flag for my books. You all continue to help gluten-free people find my books and for that, I am forever grateful.

Thank you so much to my boyfriend, recipe tester and proofreader, Mark, who is infinitely supportive despite never signing up for the last two roles! Thanks to my dog and mini mascot, Peggy, who has probably been awoken by the beeping sound of an air fryer more than any dog ever should over the last few months.

Thank you sincerely to my mum and dad for always supporting me and being far too understanding that I basically have zero time!

Thanks again to my brother Charlie, Gemma and the Farrow clan, as well as Mark's mum, dad and sister, Lisa, and her partner Michael, for all the constant support, recipe testing and positivity.

Thank you as always to Nigella Lawson for her constant support and kindness ever since I released my first book. I'm not sure she knows how much I truly appreciate it or how her extremely flattering words on the cover of this book have led to everyone often actually calling me the 'Queen of gluten-free!' I think we all know Nigella is the real Queen here!

A huge thank you to my Facebook group moderators Lizzie, Sharon, Bindu, Amanda, Kirstie, Debbie (and Cole!), CJ, Sandie and Gina. Honestly, with the rate things keep growing, I absolutely couldn't run the Facebook group without you! Please remember that, as volunteers, you absolutely shouldn't feel like there is an expectation to do so!

And finally, thanks a million to all my dedicated followers/readers (especially those of you in the Facebook group) for the constant love and support across all of my books so far. The creation of this book was largely due to listening to your comments, and you guys absolutely deserve credit for that. Thank you for your persistent guidance and motivation to keep writing books like this one!

**Managing Director**
Sarah Lavelle

**Commissioning and Project Editor**
Harriet Webster

**Copy Editor**
Sally Somers

**Art Direction and Design**
Emily Lapworth

**Designer**
Nikki Ellis

**Photographer**
Hannah Hughes

**Food Stylist**
Amy Stephenson

**Prop Stylist**
Max Robinson

**Make-up Artist**
Cat Parnell

**Head of Production**
Stephen Lang

**Senior Production Controller**
Sabeena Atchia

First published in 2024 by Quadrille Publishing Limited

Quadrille
52–54 Southwark Street
London SE1 1UN
quadrille.com

Cataloguing in Publication Data:
a catalogue record for this book
is available from the British Library.

ISBN: 978 1 83783 243 9

Printed in China

Many thanks to **Ninja**, **Lakeland**, **Salter**,
**Russell Hobbs**, **Tower** and **Zwilling**, who
kindly donated air fryers for the photoshoot.

**Disclaimer:** This book is not intended as a substitute
for genuine medical advice. The reader should consult
a medical professional in matters relating to their
health, particularly with regard to symptoms of IBS
and coeliac disease.

FODMAP information was correct at the time of
writing, but please check the Monash University
FODMAP app for the latest information on serving
sizes. These may change via updates in the future.

MIX
Paper | Supporting
responsible forestry
FSC™ C020056
FSC www.fsc.org